D0411093

The Evolution of Victory

THE EVOLUTION OF VICTORY

British Battles on the Western Front
1914-1918

Andy Simpson

Tom Donovan
London

First published in 1995 by

Tom Donovan Publishing Ltd.
52 Willow Road
Hampstead
London NW3 1TP

ISBN: 1-871085-19-5

© 1995 Tom Donovan Publishing Ltd. & A. Simpson

All rights reserved. No part of this publication may be reproduced, stored
in a retrieval system or transmitted in any form, by any means, electrical,
mechanical or otherwise, without first seeking the written permission of
the copyright owner and of the publisher.

Desk-top typeset by Tom Donovan Publishing Ltd.

Printed by The Bath Press, Bath

UNIVERSITY
OF
GLASGOW
LIBRARY

To my Mother

Acknowledgements

The author would like to acknowledge the benefit of numerous discussions with the following which have contributed materially to this book: Peter Simkins; Chris McCarthy; Bryn Hammond; Paul Harris; Tom Donovan. Any errors or omissions are the responsibility of the author alone.

Contents

Maps

Illustrations

Fifteen photographs will be found between pages 88-89. All photographs, with the exceptions of numbers 4 and 11 are reproduced by kind permission of the Trustees of the Imperial War Museum, London.

Introduction

This book is an attempt to show how the British army, and the technology applied by it, changed over the course of the First World War. It does not purport to be a complete history of the war, or to examine the war in the air or at Westminster, except from time to time as they impinged on the land fighting. The war at sea is not mentioned at all. Nor are fronts other than the Western considered. Notwithstanding the lives tragically lost at Gallipoli and in the Middle East and elsewhere, the main focus of the fighting for the British lay in Belgium and northwest France. This necessarily leads to some distortions; the part played by the naval blockade in bringing about Germany's defeat, for example, is not discussed.

It is hoped that this work will do something to show that the 'donkeys' who led the British Expeditionary Force were prepared to accept the introduction of technological and tactical change on an unprecedented scale, as long as it helped them breach the German defences. The techniques introduced in 1914-18 for controlling artillery fire were not surpassed until 1942, and the intensity of the latter in 1918 not exceeded by the British army until 1945. The lower casualties in the Second World War are used as a stick with which to beat the generals of the First; but in the later war the Sommes and Passchendaeles took place on the Eastern Front between 1941 and 1945. The Soviet Union alone lost more than twenty times as many lives in the Second World War as did the British Empire in the First.

The format is of analyses of important engagements, from planning to execution, interspersed with what it is hoped are illuminating anecdotes from participants' letters, diaries and memoirs. Spelling and punctuation are left as in the originals, which occasionally leads to peculiarities of both. If, at times, it seems that a battle is described more superficially than those before or after, it is because space precludes a detailed discussion of everything, and if technological or tactical innovation was more pronounced in one battle than another, the former is dealt with in more detail. A glossary is provided at the back of the book, in order to clarify technical terms and abbreviations not explained in the text. Finally, the convention used in the Official History of italicising the names of German units is followed; it is hoped that this will help to avoid confusion.

1
The Old Order:
Mons to First Ypres

The Great War on the Western Front began with Germany and France putting into effect their respective plans for each other's defeat. The German Schlieffen Plan had originally been conceived towards the end of the previous century, by the Chief of the Great General Staff of that name. It relied on delivering a swift knock-out blow to France, before her Russian ally could mobilize and embroil Germany in a war on two fronts. Put simply, the right wing of the German armies would be massively stronger than the left, and would sweep through Belgium and northern France, in a huge enveloping movement, passing south of Paris and ultimately smashing the French forces against their eastern border. If the French chose to attack there, in order to regain the provinces of Alsace and Lorraine (lost after the Franco-Prussian War of 1870-1) so much the better. The German left would give ground in order to lure their opponents more tightly into the trap. While the plan was modified after von Schlieffen's death, this was still more or less its form in 1914 - though it was to be drastically altered in practice by von Moltke, the Chief of Staff in 1914.

The French Plan XVII (so called because it was the 17th to be adopted since the end of the Franco-Prussian War) was a reflection of the conventional view in French military circles that the offensive would always prevail over the defensive. Since a plan like Schlieffen's would require enormous manpower, which the French did not believe the Germans possessed (not realising the intention of the latter to use reservists as well as first-line troops), they must attack through Lorraine or the Ardennes. Two French armies would therefore pour into Lorraine, and then on to the Saar. Another two, to the left, would advance across the border further west and through the Ardennes, while one more would act as a strategic reserve.

The British Expeditionary Force set off for France, under its commander, Sir John French, two corps strong, and comprising some 100,000 men. Staff talks between the French and British armies before the war had always been unofficial, and so there were no clear and explicit instructions regarding the BEF's role in the fighting to come, other than that it was to position itself on the left flank of the French 5th Army and assist in the advance against the invading Germans.

After disembarkation at the ports of Boulogne, Rouen and Le Havre between 12th and 17th August, it moved to concentrate at Maubeuge, just south of the Franco-Belgian border (and, as planned, on the extreme left flank of the French). Upon advancing further, it encamped for the night of 22nd August in and around the industrial town of Mons. Sir John French intended to advance again on the following day, notwithstanding intelligence reports of German infantry columns moving towards him, preceded by cavalry patrols which the BEF's cavalry had already encountered. However, reports from liaison officers made it clear that this would not be possible, for the commander of the neighbouring French 5th Army, which was sorely pressed by German attacks, had decided that it must retreat on the 23rd. Any advance by the BEF would therefore invite its envelopment and destruction by the Germans. Consequently, Sir John declined his ally's suggestion that he continue to press forward, but in the interests of inter-allied co-operation agreed to support the 5th Army by making a stand at Mons for 24 hours.

This decision came as a shock to the Germans of *1st Army* (the extreme right wing of the attack) under General von Kluck, who had expected to meet only a few cavalry picquets, to be easily brushed aside. Instead, they met stiff opposition from the British troops, protected by hastily constructed entrenchments and barricades running east-west along the line of the Mons-Condé canal (principally held by II Corps) and on the right along a line running south-east in order to protect the right flank of the position (principally held by I Corps). The left flank was covered by French troops. The dense columns of German troops, attacking in the formations which had served them so well against the French in 1870 were unmissable targets for the skilled riflemen of the BEF.[1]

---

[1]   The British army had fought a full-scale war far more recently than either the French or the Germans. The war in South Africa (1899-1902) had revealed the shortcomings of massed formations in the face of modern weaponry, and also the relative ineffectiveness of British musketry. In consequence, and because of governmental reluctance to provide a large enough budget for the army to have as many machine-guns as it wanted, far more attention had been paid to musketry training in the years 1902-14 than before.

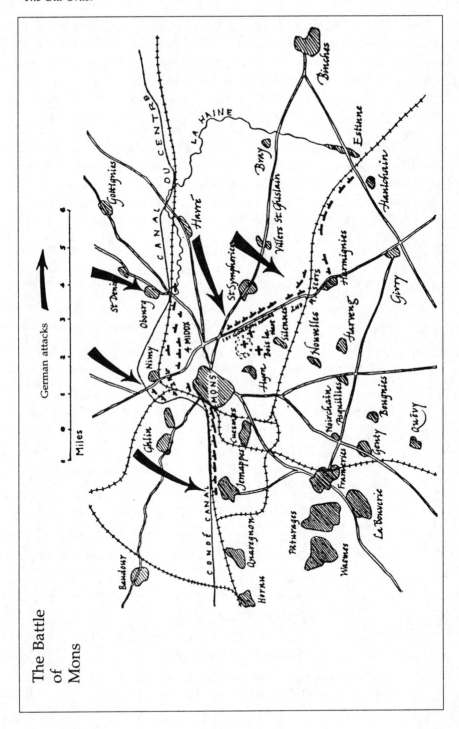

The Battle
of
Mons

German attacks →

Miles

The German attacks were concentrated against II Corps' front, and especially the salient formed at the right of its line by the curve of the canal around Mons itself. Meeting with heavy casualties and little success, despite their considerable artillery superiority, by the end of the day some of the German commanders actually feared British counter-attacks. However, these fears were unfounded, as under the weight of the attacks in the afternoon the situation in the salient had become confused, and with pressure mounting on the left of I Corps, II Corps' commander, Sir Horace Smith-Dorrien, felt obliged to withdraw to a shorter and more defensible position. II Corps had suffered almost all of the day's 1,600 casualties, and the figure was at the time believed to be higher. The last important attack of the day fell on the 1st Gordon Highlanders and 2nd Royal Scots, on the extreme left of I Corps, adjacent to the salient mentioned before:

> The trench, three feet deep and not much more than eighteen inches broad, formed a gradual curve thirty to forty yards in length, and sheltered three sections of the platoon. The fourth section was entrenched on higher ground a hundred yards back, protecting our left flank... The German shells came in bunches; some burst over the road behind, others yet farther away crashed into the woods of Hyon. At the same time the rattle of one of our machine-guns on the left and the sound of rapid rifle fire from the same quarter showed that C Company had found a target, while as yet we peered over our trenches in vain. I will not pretend to give an account of the battle of Mons, "because you have better in the prints," and because my confused recollection of what took place during the rest of the afternoon will not permit of recounting in their due order even events which took place on our small part of the front. The noise of bursting shells, the sound of hard fighting on our left, must have endured for nearly an hour before any attempt was made by the Germans, now swarming in the wood behind the white house, to leave cover and make an attack on our front. From the farthest point of the wood, at a range of 1200 yards, a large body of troops marched out into the open in column, moving across our front to our left flank, evidently for the purpose of reinforcing the attack on C Company.
>
> At 1200 yards rifle fire, even at such a target, is practically useless. It was impossible to resist the temptation to open fire with the hope of breading up the column formation and thus delaying the reinforcement operations. "No. 1 Section, at 1200 yards, three rounds rapid." I bent over the parapet, glasses fixed on the column. They were not quite clear of the wood and marching along as if on parade.
>
> At the first volley the column halted, some of the men skipped into the wood and most of them turned and faced in our direction. With the

second and third volleys coming in rapid succession they rushed in a body for cover.

All our shots seemed to have gone too high and none found a billet, but the enemy made no further attempt to leave the wood in close formation, but presently advanced along the edge of the wood in single file, marching in the same direction as before, and affording no target at such a distance.

Various descriptions of the battle of Mons speak of the Germans advancing like grey clouds covering the earth, of "massed formation" moving across the open to within close range of our trenches, to be decimated by "murderous fire."

On every extended battle line incidents will occur affording opportunities for picturesque writing, but in the attack and defence of an open position in the days of pre-trench war, excepting always the noise of bursting shells, the hum of bullets and the absence of umpires, the whole affair is a passable imitation of a field-day in peace time.

Our position at Hyon, important because it dominated the line of retreat, was weakly held. We had practically no supports. The German superiority at that part of the line was probably about three to one in guns, and five or more to one in men.

The enemy attacked vigorously, met with an unexpectedly vigorous resistance, hesitated, failed to push their action home, and lost an opportunity which seldom occurred again - an opportunity which has now gone for ever... The steady hammer of one of our machine-guns and a renewed burst of rapid fire from the rifles of C Company made it clear that an attack on the village was in progress. Then the battery whose first shell had nearly dropped into our trench put their second shot neatly on to the red-tiled house at the left-hand corner of the village...

Twenty feet above the red tiles a double flash like the twinkling of a great star, a graceful puff of smoke, soft and snow-white like cotton-wool. In that second the red tiles vanished and nothing of the roof remained but the bare rafters.

Now our guns were searching out the German artillery positions, and sent shell after shell far over our heads on to the distant woods; and now the German shells, outnumbering ours by two or three to one, were bursting all along the woods behind our trenches and behind the main road. The noise of what was after all a very mild bombardment [by later standards] seemed very terrible to our unaccustomed ears!

Still the rattle of a machine-gun on our left; but the bursts of rifle fire were less prolonged and at rarer intervals, so that the pressure of the German attack was apparently relaxing. The surprise of the day came from our right flank.

Here the main road ran across and away diagonally from our line, so that the amount of open ground in front of No. 14 Trench was considerably nearer 600 than 400 yards - the whole distance from this trench to the road being bare pasture-land, with scarcely cover for a rabbit. No. 14 Trench extends to within a few yards of the thick plantation which runs almost parallel with our line. The cover is not much more than two or three acres in extent, and on the far side of the wood the line is carried on by another company.

I was on the point of laying down my glasses, having made a final sweep of the ground, including a look down to No. 14 Trench, when something caught my attention in the plantation, and at that same moment a body of troops in extended order dashed out of the woods and doubled across the open meadow. The sight of these men, coming apparently from behind our own line and making at such speed for the enemy, was so entirely unexpected that, although their uniforms even at the long range seemed unfamiliar, I did not realise they were Germans. A volley from No. 14 Trench put an end to uncertainty. The line broke, each man running for safety at headlong speed; here and there a man, dropping backwards, lay still on the grass.

In the centre of the line the officer, keeping rather behind the rest, stumbled and fell. The two men nearest him stopped, bent down to assist him, looking for a moment anxiously into his face as he lay back on the grass, then quickly turned and ran for cover. A very few seconds more and the remaining racing figures dodged between trees on the main road and found safety.

When the rifle fire ceased, two or three of the grey bodies dotted about the field were seen to move; one or two rose up and staggered a few paces, only to fall at once and lie motionless; another two or three wriggled and crawled away; and one rose up apparently unhurt, running in zigzag fashion, dodging from side to side with sudden cunning, though no further shot was fired.

The German attack now began to press on both flanks - on the left perhaps with less vigour, but on the right an ever-increasing intensity of rifle fire seemed to come almost from behind our trenches; but on neither left nor right could anything be seen of the fighting. The ceaseless tapping of our two machine-guns was anxious hearing during that long afternoon, and in the confusion of bursting shells the sound of busy rifles seemed to be echoing on all sides.

Three German officers stepped out from the edge of the wood behind the white house; they stood out in the open, holding a map and discussing together the plan of attack. The little group seemed amazingly near in the mirror of my field-glass, but afforded too hopelessly small a target for rifle fire at a thousand yards' range. The conference was, however, cut short by a shell from our faithful battery behind the wood of Hyon. A few minutes later, the officers having skipped back into cover, a long line of the now familiar grey coats advanced slowly about ten yards from the wood and lay down in the beetroot field; an officer, slightly in front of his men, carrying a walking-stick and remaining standing until another shell threw him on his face with the rest.

Our shells were bursting splendidly beyond the white house, with now and then a shell on what had once been the red-tiled corner house, and now and then a shell into the woods beyond where the German reserves were sheltering.

Two or three lines of supports issued forth from the wood, and the first line pushed close up to the white house; but as long as we could see to shoot, and while our shells were sprinkling the fields with shrapnel, the enemy failed to reach their objective and suffered heavy casualties.

After the sun had set the vigour of the fight was past, and in the twilight few shells were exchanged from wood to wood, although machine-guns still drummed and rifles cracked, keeping the enemy from further advance. [Lt. M.V.Hay, 1st Gordon Highlanders]

The BEF had been attacked by a force of at least 200,000 men, although by no means all had been committed; on the day, both sides' commanders conspicuously failed to control the battle. Given that the French were continuing to fall back under heavy German pressure, there was no alternative for the BEF but to disengage and retreat. The chiefs of staff of the two corps were summoned to GHQ, 35 miles away, for a meeting in the small hours of the night of 23rd/24th August, and orders were issued for retreat. J.E. Gough, of I Corps, had the sensible idea of telegraphing them through to Sir Douglas Haig, his commander, and so the latter was able to issue his own orders at 2a.m. and have the corps away by 5a.m. Gough's counterpart in II Corps, George Forestier-Walker, did not have the same idea and instead travelled the 35 miles back to corps HQ before telling Smith-Dorrien at about 3a.m. of the orders. Consequently, II Corps became involved in further fighting by 7a.m. on 24th August. Although it extricated itself, Smith-Dorrien was concerned that his men were exhausted after the previous day's fighting and so met Haig at noon to request that I Corps cover his retirement. However, friction between the two corps commanders and to a larger extent between their chiefs of staff meant that, I Corps having moved so much earlier than II, Haig was unwilling or unable to oblige.

GHQ seemed incapable of exercising effective authority, and the two corps diverged as they fell back. From 26th August to 1st September they were completely out of touch with one another, initially separated by the obstacle of the Forest of Mormal. On the former date, Smith-Dorrien decided to make a stand at Le Cateau. This was against GHQ's orders, but he was convinced that further retreat would lead to the destruction of his command, for it was far more closely pressed by the Germans than I Corps. While it has been suggested that he disobeyed orders, in fact he exercised the prerogative of the commander on the spot to use his own judgement when he came to his decision.

Although controversial, the stand at Le Cateau is now considered to have saved the BEF as a whole. Such was the setback his troops suffered in the battle that von Kluck thought that he had engaged both corps and a number of French divisions, rather than the three infantry and one cavalry divisions at Smith-Dorrien's disposal. The pursuit of the BEF had been delayed for a crucial twelve hours, and when it recommenced was conducted only by inconsiderable forces. II Corps' achievement was fully recognised soon afterwards in Sir John French's despatch, and as the Official History later stated:

> 'With both flanks more or less in the air, [II Corps] had turned upon an enemy of at least twice their strength; had struck him hard, and had withdrawn... practically without interference, with neither flank enveloped, having suffered losses certainly severe, but considering the circumstances, by no means extravagant.'

Despite the Germans' numerical superiority, the rate and accuracy of the British regulars' rifle fire again won the day, as recounted to Frederick Coleman, a civilian volunteer attached to the BEF:

> ...a couple of South Lancs men entered. One of the pair was voluble enough for both. He was eager to explain the whole battle. He drew the 2nd Corps' position in line and placed the Germans in a half circle, the ends flanking the British right and left.

> "We were well entrenched," he said, "and the Germans opened on us from five hundred to six hundred yards. They fire in absolute masses. Never was anything like it heard of. One row of them lies down, behind them a row kneels, and back of them again a third row stands. You couldn't imagine such a target. It seemed too easy. You could just pump the bullets into 'em like smoke, and never miss a shot. You have no idea how it seemed, lying there firing into that grey bunch of men and thinking all the time what fools they were to stand there and take it. And the funny thing was that they couldn't shoot for nuts either. The

standing lot didn't even raise their rifles to their shoulders, but fired from the hip. The must have sent an awful lot of pills our way, but they couldn't hit a balloon."

The quieter soldier took up the narrative. "As fast as we would knock over a German another would take his place."

That had impressed both of the South Lancs men. They spoke of that feature of the fight with obvious respect for the men, fools and Germans though they were, who could stand such punishment.

"Our men must have hit at least ten of them to every one of us that got it," said the quiet one.

Both men were loud in the praise of our guns, the fire from which had been splendidly accurate. "But that battery back of us got it like hell afterwards."

With the final comments of the two soldiers above in mind, the artillery performance of the British deserves consideration. It should be noted that artillery fire can be divided into three types: direct, indirect and predicted. The last will be dealt with elsewhere in this book. Direct fire is that occurring when a gun is within sight of its target and the fall of shot can be observed by the gun-aimer. Indirect fire is used when a gun is out of view of its target, for instance when the former is on the reverse slope of a hill and the latter in the valley on the other side of the crest. An observer is required to report the fall of shot back to the gun crew in order to let them adjust their aim accordingly. Prewar debate over the relative merits of the two types of fire, the product of experience in the Boer War and observation in the Russo-Japanese War (1904-5) had wavered between the two. Infantrymen were generally in favour of direct fire though gunners viewed indirect as more effective. In the event, direct fire was only rarely employed after Le Cateau.

Its use then was for two principal reasons. Firstly, it was then felt that the artillery should be seen to be in close support of the infantry, and secondly, given the relatively ineffective use of machine-guns in the BEF as compared to the German army, the latter's superiority had to be compensated for by shrapnel fire at close range. However, the greater numbers of the German artillery meant that the British suffered heavily, not least when firing or pulling their guns back when within only a few hundred yards of the enemy. In fact, those batteries employing indirect fire were the more effective on the day.

The German superiority in numbers of artillery pieces was augmented by their having proportionately far more medium and heavy guns and howitzers. In contrast to later thought, irrespective of

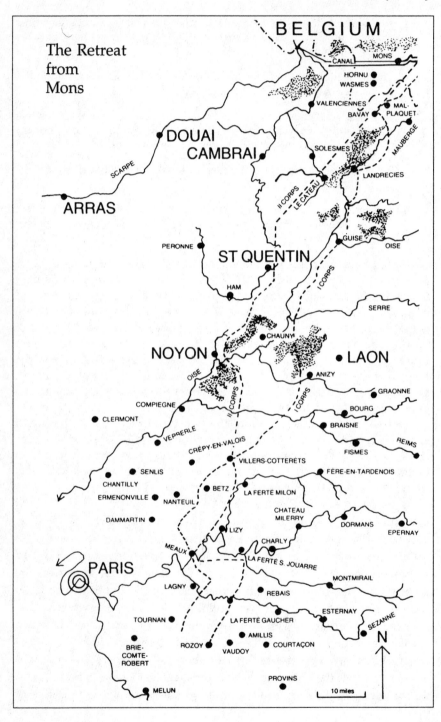

The Retreat
from
Mons

BELGIUM

CANAL
MONS
HORNU
WASMES
VALENCIENNES
BAVAY
MAL-
PLAQUET
MAUBERGE
DOUAI
CAMBRAI
SOLESMES
LANDRECIES
SCARPE
II CORPS
LE CATEAU
ARRAS
GUISE
OISE
PERONNE
ST QUENTIN
HAM
I CORPS
SERRE
CHAUNY
NOYON
LAON
OISE
ANIZY
GRAONNE
COMPIEGNE
II CORPS
BOURG
CLERMONT
BRAISNE
I CORPS
VERBERIE
REIMS
CRÉPY-EN-VALOIS
FISMES
VILLERS-COTTERETS
SENLIS
FÈRE-EN-TARDENOIS
CHANTILLY
BETZ
LA FERTÉ MILON
ERMENONVILLE
NANTEUIL
CHATEAU
MILERRY
DAMMARTIN
DORMANS
EPERNAY
LIZY
CHARLY
MEAUX
LA FERTÉ S. JOUARRE
PARIS
MONTMIRAIL
LAGNY
REBAIS
ESTERNAY
TOURNAN
SEZANNE
LA FERTÉ GAUCHER
N
ROZOY
AMILLIS
BRIE-
COMTE-
ROBERT
VAUDOY
COURTAÇON
PROVINS
MELUN
10 miles

the type of fire used, the British army's doctrine was that the role of the artillery was principally to support the infantry attack; consequently, at the start of the war, light, shrapnel-firing guns were in the great majority in the BEF. An infantry division had 54 of these 18-pounders, as compared to 18 4.5" howitzers and only four 60-pounder guns; while the fewer still heavier guns in service were obsolete and in any case not even sent to France until the end of September. The need to destroy enemy trenches, or at least to kill their occupants had not been foreseen. Subsequent fighting was to cause radical changes in the army's thinking and in the relationship between infantry and artillery.

Notwithstanding the beneficial consequences of Le Cateau, the retreat continued until 6th September. At times, considerable confusion reigned - it being always an extremely difficult job to hold a retreating army together. The difficulty of retaining contact even with one's own unit is illustrated in the following extract:

> Shortly after daylight the train dribbled into a station. Nobody came to meet it. Master, rubbing his eyes, sprang from the carriage and looked about him. This certainly was not Amiens, and yet we were due there hours before. The place was as deserted as Berlaiment. At last a senior Staff officer (medical) was discovered sitting alone near the telegraph station.
>
> 'What are you doing here?' inquired the latter anxiously.
>
> 'We started for Amiens,' answered Master. 'The engine brought us here apparently.'
>
> 'Well, it brought you wrong,' came the firm answer. 'This is Noyon, and no place to loiter in, unless you want to be captured. If you were told to go to Amiens, you had better go.'
>
> Master grunted his feelings. Things began to look as if we were running. Like a dog with his tail between his legs, he sauntered up the platform, seeking possible news. Presently he discovered a solitary figure leaning disconsolately against a station-house. Closer observation disclosed a dirty, unkempt, young medical officer.
>
> 'Who are you?' asked Master.
>
> 'Medical officer of the — regiment.'
>
> 'What has happened? Where is the regiment?'
>
> 'Don't know,' answered the youngster wearily. 'The Colonel gave the order to retire, and I retired with them.' He rubbed his three days' beard and paused to control his shaking voice. 'They scattered. I lost them. I

believe they are - er - all killed.'

Some distance further along, a young infantry private dragged himself into the station and sank down on a box. We spoke to him, anxiously seeking news. He was but an honest English lad who had evidently not been long from the country. He stared vacantly to his front. He tried to answer our questions, but his voice broke in a sob. We realised what the shock must have been to him. He had indeed seen war. We left him, and hurried, with chastened spirits, back to our truck. [Col. F.A.Symons, RAMC].

As the BEF and the French 5th Army continued to fall back in the direction of Paris, von Kluck's *1st Army* began to outstrip its neighbour, the *2nd Army*. By the end of August he had been ordered by the German supreme command (which viewed the BEF and 5th Army as spent) to rein in his advance and to keep in echelon with *2nd Army* to his left, pushing the British and French south-east, away from Paris. In this way, it was hoped that he could protect the German right against French forces assembling to the east of their capital. However, when this order reached him on 3rd September, von Kluck's men were already 12 miles ahead of *2nd Army*. He reasoned that if he let up the pressure on the BEF and 5th Army, they would be given a breathing space in which to regroup and co-ordinate their efforts with the French to the east of Paris. And given the impossibility of adhering to the Schlieffen Plan's concept of enveloping the latter, owing to the exhaustion of his men and the lack of troops to invest it in any case (von Moltke having diverted men to the left wing and the Eastern Front), he decided to ignore the order and to press on as fast as possible. However, on the next day he began to realise that he was dangerously isolated; *2nd Army* was now 14 miles behind and he was receiving intelligence reports of British and French troops deployed in large numbers to the south, south-east and west (i.e. covering Paris) of his Army. Unknown to him, aerial reconnaissance had revealed to the Allies that the moment had come for counter-attack. On 6th September the Battle of the Marne began, the French pressing eastward from Paris and northward from the Seine (further to the east). In between these forces, the British attacked north-east, moving into the gap between *1st* and *2nd Armies*, which was held only by a cavalry division and an infantry brigade. Frederick Coleman, attached to the Cavalry Division of the BEF, witnessed some of the fighting on 7th September, as this gap was exploited:

Colonel Seely materialized during the afternoon, and gave us news that Pulteney's 3rd Corps[formed in the field on 31st August] was fighting hard on our left, and the French on our right were fiercely engaged and forging slowly forward.

We bivouacked that night in the fields, dining in the stubble by the headlights of the car, and sleeping in the open. A chilly night after the hot day, and wet.

Four o'clock on the morning of Monday, the 7th saw us up and warming ourselves by the welcome fire, over which breakfast coffee was boiling.

Moving on, the objective of our column, one of three lines of cavalry, was in the general direction of La Ferté Gaucher again, leaving Choisy on our left. Conneau's [French] cavalry was close at hand on our right, and keeping line with us.

A wrong turning at a cross-road put me in advance of the 2nd Brigade.

I ran into a bit of sniping fire, but it soon ceased as our advance guard went forward. We were in touch with the enemy every foot of the way, though we had not as yet found him in force. Seven or eight Uhlans rode from behind a cluster of stacks, less than a thousand yards from us, and galloped to the north, a handful of our troopers hotfoot after them. Then heavy rifle fire in front, and, soon after, our guns.

Oh, the fascination of it! The glory of a galloping regiment of cavalry, flowing over a green field in line of squadrons! On we pushed. Past a little village in a valley, tucked away so cleverly one came upon it unawares, then on to a rise of ground, another dip, then a steep hill, and suddenly a shell burst right in front. I pulled up short. The fascination of it was like to run away with me when our own cavalry was chasing the German cavalry. Also it was like to run away with my judgment. A car [Coleman was a civilian volunteer driver] might get further forward than necessary, perhaps even further forward than was wise.

Bang! bang! Two German shrapnel. Whizz, over and beyond, with a bang behind. Crash! One fell to the right, between two squads of galloping troopers. The horses reared and shied, but not one fell. The second group rode through the white shell-cloud, and dashed on.

Rifle fire ahead, and bang came a shell, bursting over me. Bang! Much too close!

I went into the village of Montcel to seek the protection of its buildings, leaving the car.

I passed up the wide street, deserted except by a dead German officer in front of a cottage, and gained the further edge of the cluster of mean houses that composed the village.

Behind a friendly stone wall, I stopped and took out my [field-]glasses.

The stubble stretched away towards a line of woods.

Diagonally across the broad road that led north from the village, came a line of horsemen.

Magnificent in the morning sun they rode, a solid line rising and falling with regular cadence, as though mechanically propelled.

The 1st Garde Dragoner Regiment of Berlin, of the Garde Cavallerie Division of the Garde Corps, the proudest, finest cavalry of the German Army - over one hundred of them, seeming double the number to me - were charging across the fields.

On they came, like machine-made waves on a machine-made ocean.

Then from the left shot other horsemen, one well ahead, another not far back, and a scattered scurrying bunch of two score behind, riding like mad, full tilt at the ranks of German pride and might bearing down upon them.

Colonel David Campbell, of the 9th Lancers, close on his heels Captain Reynolds, his adjutant, and forty-five of his gallant regiment were charging more than double their number of the flower of the enemy's horse.

The Germans quickened appreciably, and their lances waved downwards to the rest. Their pace was slow compared with the whirlwind rush of the smaller band.

I was on the wall when the impact came. Crash! went the 9th into the Garde. Colonel Campbell and Captain Reynolds were down, and horses reared and staggered. I wondered that none of the chargers funked it. Each horse seemed imbued with the spirit of his rider. Not one charger "refused."

No sooner had the smash come that I realised the wall was no place for me, so off I dashed to my car and safety.

The 9th scored heavily off their more numerous foes. A few fell, but more than double the number of Germans bit the dust. Crack British troopers proved their undoubted superiority, man for man, by the number of German dead and wounded we found on the field. Galloping on, the 9th circled round the village and away to the rear... By this time Colonel Burnett, of the 18th Hussars, with a dismounted squadron, had worked round to the left with a machine-gun. When he opened on then, the Germans mounted and swung by him and into the full line of fire.

That squadron of the 18th had a splendid target.

Although the Franco-British attacks met with less success than had been hoped for, they constituted enough of a setback for the Germans, with their lines of communication over-extended and their troops consequently short of supplies, to fall back on 9th September. Notwithstanding Coleman's enthusiasm for the dash of the cavalry, the BEF was handled timidly at this point and the retiring Germans were not closely pressed. Nevertheless,the Battle of the Marne spelled the ruin of Germany's prewar strategy; France had not been defeated in the planned 40 days, and Germany was left with the much-feared war on two fronts. Captain R.V.Dolbey, Medical Officer of 2nd King's Own Scottish Borderers, gives an indication of the disarray in which the Germans retreated:

> The story of the German retreat was written all along the road. They discarded from weakness as a man does from his hand at bridge. First, were innumerable wine bottles, all empty; then full bottles lying smashed in the ditches by the roadside, and boxes of cigars. Pictures, some cut from their frames, others intact, leant drunkenly against the hedges. Stationery half buried in the roadside vegetation. The transport was hard pushed to have to abandon the loot of many French châteaux; the officers' loot withal. Then curious specimens of plunder appeared, hanging on the roadside hedges, trampled in the mud - the loot the marching infantry alone could take by reason of its lightness, women's gear, soft frilly things, which the simple German soldier was taking home to his wife, so light to carry and so eminently French. Then transport horses, shot and methodically stripped of saddlery and shoes; later, we came upon poor beasts, dead, but with shoes intact; then horses, still methodically shot, so as to rob us of any possible future use of them, but with saddlery left on - merely cut from the traces. The pursuit was growing fiercer, and the plight of the wheeled transport was at every mile, more urgent. Farther on, by the roadside, with hanging heads and bent trembling knees, were abandoned horses which there had been no time to shoot or strip; some standing, others too foundered to rise. The dead animals blocked the pursuit, their bellies so swollen with gas that their legs stuck out at an angle with their bodies. Then came the abandoned wagons themselves. Flour, a bright yellow pea flour for making the universal soup, was lying in bright ochreous patches all along the line of retreat; harness, sausage machines, cutlery, cooks' gear - all abandoned. Evidence of the thorough work of the German regimental butchers was here; first, whole carcasses, carefully skinned, had been thrown away; later, as the pace grew hotter, quarters of meat methodically and neatly jointed.

> So frantic was their haste, that, when we would come to the narrow stone bridges that crossed the streams at the foot of little valleys, we could see where three transport wagons had raced to get first to the bridge. They had met and jammed between the parapets and blocked the road. Then we saw where they had been lifted over the parapets and

thrown into the stream below; drowned horses and upturned wagons in the water.

This retreat was worse conducted than our own from Le Cateau; for there we got our transport well away ahead, so that the roads were not blocked for infantry and artillery. Here the Germans had kept their transport back too late, and every road was indescribably jumbled with guns, infantry, motorcars, and wagons. This was by far the most satisfactory day the Expeditionary Force had seen since war began, and compensated in a large measure for our retreat from Mons.

The BEF, having advanced across the River Marne in the face of minimal opposition on 8th/9th September, pushed north-east until on the 12th, I Corps reached the River Aisne, having in seven days marched 70 miles and captured more than 1,000 prisoners. Sir Douglas Haig paused at this obstacle, preferring to delay his advance until joined by II Corps on his left. At 8a.m. on 13th September, the advance guards of I Corps moved up to the river itself, in preparation for the crossing which took place later that day. To the left of II Corps was III Corps, elements of which were able to press across the river late on 12th September. Lt. the Hon. Lionel Tennyson, acting as Orderly Officer to Br.-Gen. Aylmer Hunter-Weston (commanding 11th Infantry Brigade), recorded this advance guard's crossing and the subsequent fighting:

> On the night of the 12th, after an awful march of twenty-seven miles still in torrents of rain to the village of Roziérés, we were ordered to advance once more just as we got ready to billet for the night, and arrived after yet another drenching at Venizel on the River Aisne.

> That night the whole of the 11th Brigade crossed the river. This was the manner of their crossing, which at the time seemed to us the riskiest and most slap-dash proceeding ever seen. The Germans had meant to destroy the bridge, but had left a single girder standing on the left side. In the midst of the inky darkness, and although the men were so tired with their forty miles march in the rain that they went to sleep as they stood or marched, they crossed this girder one by one. It was sixty feet above the river and quivered and shook all the time. As soon as all were across (and for some reason not a shot had been fired by the enemy) the whole Brigade passed through the village of Bucy-le-Long to the summit of the ridge beyond. Though the Battle of the Aisne lasted three weeks, this was the farthest point reached by our Brigade. There Germans were strongly entrenched with artillery some five hundred to eight hundred yards to our front and it was impossible to get on. On the afternoon of the first day, Sunday 13th, after my Company [of Tennyson's battalion, 1st Rifle Brigade] had by mistake been shelled by our own guns in the morning and lost a dozen men, killed and wounded, A and B companies

were, it is true, ordered to advance, but were soon compelled to retire after heavy casualties, which included three officers wounded...

After this reverse we started entrenching and were heavily shelled from 5 a.m. to 10 a.m., during which time I was hit by a spent piece of shell but not injured. After a lull in the firing I was astonished to see our Colonel, Biddulph, and Sir Evelyn Bradford, the old Hampshire cricketer, who commanded the Seaforths, come up in the open behind our trenches and call out Jimmy Brownlow my captain. They all three stood looking at a map and I heard the words "General Advance." At that moment two shells burst in rapid succession right by them. Bradford was instantly killed and Brownlow desperately wounded, though he eventually recovered, but our Colonel only had his cap blown off...

Every day the shelling grew more violent, and we were continually losing men as the Germans were using very heavy guns. We therefore dug and improved our trenches each night. Battalion headquarters were in some caves in the wood behind our lines.

The rest of the BEF crossed on the following day. II Corps began later than I and III and consequently encountered heavier opposition; other means than damaged bridges were sometimes required to get across the river:

Soon the machine-gun fire became almost continuous and rapid fire rolled up and down the river banks... The temporary pontoon bridge the Engineers had put up, further down the river, had just been blown up by a shell, and the only way for me was the canvas raft that, by chance, might still be intact. The two battalions were across, he told me; there had been very many casualties he was sure; there was no doctor across the river; and he wished me luck. Telling the stretcher bearers to keep open order and take good cover, I found a practicable ditch that led to the rushes by the river bank, and gained the friendly shelter of the reeds; outwardly calm, for one of my men had plumped down near and was watching me; but inwardly trembling. A hail across the river; a subaltern of the Engineers answered me and said that the canvas raft was sinking, and would I go to the pillars of the ruined bridge; there I might shout to the Sergeant-Major, who would ferry me across. [R.V.Dolbey]

In the event, not only II Corps found German resistance stiffening on 13th September, but in accordance with the French plan for pressing forward all along the line, Sir John French ordered a further advance for 14th September, feeling that only determined and well-positioned rearguards, rather than the main body of the German forces, were facing him. But the crisis of the battle for the Germans had already passed by noon of the previous day. They had regrouped and

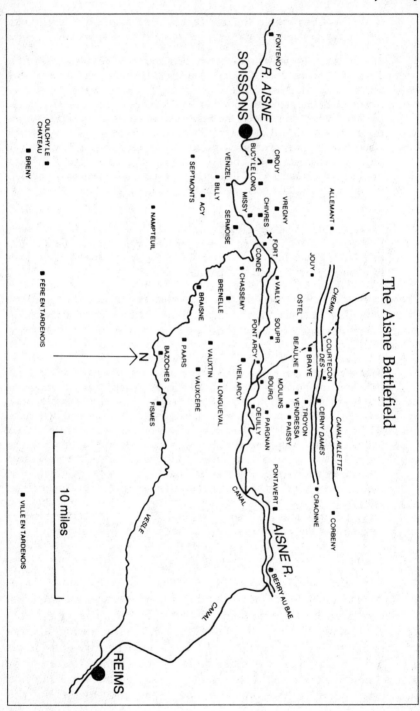

The Aisne Battlefield

reorganised their forces north of the Aisne so that General von Bülow, in command of *2nd Army*, had also had the *1st* and *7th Armies* placed under him. In addition, the German troops who had entrenched their positions on and around the Chemin des Dames ridge (which dominated the whole area of British operations) were fresh and so had not suffered the dispiriting effects of the retreat from the Marne. Not only, therefore, were they not a rearguard, but they had their own plan of attack - to throw the British advanced guards back across the river. In consequence, the BEF's advance met stiff opposition all along the front and only limited advances were made in a day of attack and counter-attack, with no decisive result for either side. Sir Douglas Haig's report on the September fighting on the Aisne stated that: 'The day's operations resulted in the gaining [of] a foothold on about 4,000 yards of front on the main ridge north of the River Aisne with strong flanking ridges covering four permanent crossings over the river. It was in fact an admirable pivot of manoeuvre for further offensive operations.' In claiming that this day's fighting had left him so well placed, Haig was perhaps making a virtue of necessity.

The reality of the situation was that the position had become more or less static; this was the start of over three years of 'siege warfare.' While the latter is not a strictly accurate description of it, trench warfare had arrived. To quote Haig's report again: 'From the 14th September the idea of immediate northward advance of the allied forces was gradually abandoned, and the line which had been gained by the 1st Corps as the result of an offensive battle had to be adapted for purposes of defence.' Once the British had entrenched themselves, he pronounced the position to be 'stronger than might have been expected', going on to say that 'although temporarily thrown on to the defensive on this line we were not prevented from undertaking local offensive action on every opportunity.' This attitude reflected the British army belief in the importance of moral[2] - or psychological - over physical factors and the need to maintain an aggressive posture whenever possible. It endured throughout the war.

Only in retrospect (Haig's report was written later, covering the period 13th-30th September) did it become apparent that no breakthrough was now possible; meanwhile, desultory operations

---

2   At times, the practice in 1914-18 was to refer to what is now called morale as 'moral.'

continued, with the artillery of both sides beginning to acquire the pre-eminent position they were to occupy later in the war. An ADC to the commander of 3rd Division reported:

> Nearly all the guns of the [3rd] Division are concealed on the plateau, and very well too. Whenever the Germans 'find' them they shift to another place, and really at present this battle had developed into an Artillery duel, nothing very fierce but a constant interchange of shots. Of course the Infantry are constantly sniping each other, but that is all that happens here for the moment."

> The roads and fields had been swept by fire all day, but our trench had been immune from all but rifle-fire. That night, however, there was a severe attack behind us, the 1st R.B.s [Rifle Brigade] being badly mauled, and the Germans got into some parts of their trench. Both they and the Somersets were much cut up, but they showed a good front to the enemy. [Captain W.LeT.Congreve]

Memorandum on British and German Tactics, written at the end of September by Haig's Chief of Staff, contains a number of pointers towards the new nature of warfare as it was to develop on the Western Front: 'our greatest difficulties have come from the enemy's machine guns and from his artillery, both of which are excellent in material and are handled with skill' and 'the German artillery is the most formidable arm we have to encounter.' His comments that the enemy 'observation of artillery fire is singularly good,' that 'observers are pushed right forward into advanced infantry trenches' and that 'the co-operation between the artillery and aeroplanes also appears to be thorough' were especially indicative of the German superiority in heavy guns at this time, and given their range, the necessity for good observation techniques. For these the aeroplane, something of an unknown quantity before the war, was already proving its worth.

One lesson which, seems not to have been readily absorbed throughout the BEF in later operations, was that it was 'necessary to revert to some of the methods which we learnt in South Africa, but which have since been forgotten... thick, regular lines of infantry' provided good targets, but 'loose and irregular elastic formations with men at 8 to 10 paces interval disposed so as to adapt themselves to any inequalities of ground suffer comparatively little, and are quite as effective as the denser formations.' While making the rather obvious point that 'infantry should be shielded as much as possible from artillery fire,' he went on to say that 'before this war it was thought that artillery bombardment unaccompanied by an infantry attack was ineffective.' He concluded that trenches should be well sited and designed and placed whenever possible on a reverse slope, even if the field of fire for the occupants was less than that of an exposed position. Furthermore, artillery should be concealed and observation posts inconspicuous and entrenched. Tentative gropings towards the immense and sophisticated barrage plans of 1917-18 can be perceived already, as Gough commented that 'there is room for improvement in our observation and control of artillery fire.' He felt that the then current system was too slow. This was that an aeroplane would spot German guns, land and report their positions to the local CRA and a staff officer, who would then arrange a time for the 'shoot' to take place. The aeroplane would then observe the fall of shot at the appointed time and radio back the results; given that the Germans were prone to moving their batteries, the inherent delay in this system was clearly unsatisfactory.

While Gough was pondering the new problems of trench warfare, Sir John French was still hoping to avoid the need for a breakthrough altogether. He decided that the emphasis of the BEF's operations would be moved north to Belgium, nearer its lines of communication to the Channel Ports and beyond the flank of the current fighting where it might then drive behind the German right wing.

The French and German armies had already begun to extend the fighting northwards in the so-called Race to the Sea, at the close of which each side made a final unsuccessful effort to turn the other's northern flank. The BEF's participation in these manoeuvres was dictated by Sir John's desire to make for himself a more independent command than he had had on the Aisne, sandwiched between French forces in static positions. However, the BEF, as it arrived from the Aisne and was augmented by a newly formed IV Corps, was put into the line piecemeal.

II Corps began to detrain at Abbeville on 8th October and went into the line west of La Bassée and north of the La Bassée canal on the 10th. On the former date IV Corps was formed around Ghent, being composed of troops sent too late to relieve the beleaguered defenders of Antwerp (the remainder of the Belgian army fell back along the coast to Nieuport, closely pressed by the Germans) and came under Sir John's command. III Corps arrived at Hazebrouck on 11th October, moving up towards Armentières, under fire, on the 13th. Meanwhile, the Cavalry Corps (formed on 10th October) had reached Messines on the 12th.

The Germans had by now changed their plan from simply

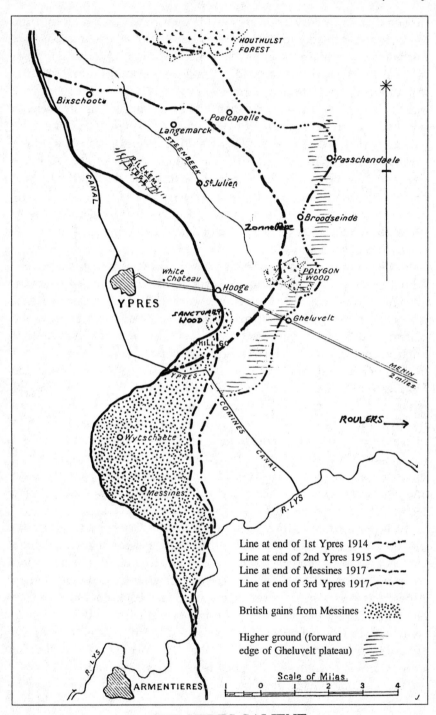

HOUTHULST
FOREST

Bixschootu

Poelcapelle

Langemarck

Passchendaele

STEENBEEK

St Julien

Broodseinde

CANAL

Zonnebeke

POLYGON
WOOD

White
Chateau

Hooge

YPRES

SANCTUARY
WOOD

Gheluvelt

HILL 60

MENIN
2 miles

YPRES

COMINES CANAL

ROULERS →

Wytschaete

R. LYS

Messines

Line at end of 1st Ypres 1914	—·—·—
Line at end of 2nd Ypres 1915	⌒⌒
Line at end of Messines 1917	—·—·—
Line at end of 3rd Ypres 1917	—···—

British gains from Messines

Higher ground (forward
edge of Gheluvelt plateau)

R. LYS

ARMENTIERES

Scale of Miles.

1   0   1   2   3   4

THE YPRES SALIENT

outflanking the Allied left to a drive on the Channel ports. Unaware of this, French, in the mistaken belief that he was not heavily opposed and that he held the initiative, on 10th October ordered all his corps to advance eastward and engage the light German screen which he thought they would encounter.

North of III Corps Hubert Gough's 2nd Cavalry Division occupied the features of Mont Noir and Mont Kemmel and forced a German withdrawal from Bailleul. By bold thrusts the Cavalry Corps had linked up with the right of IV Corps (at Wytschaete) and III, bogged down near Meteren. Further cavalry probes on the night of the 13th, however, encountered German troops in locations which British infantry were expected to have reached.

What had happened was that after their early progress, encountering only German cavalry, all attacks came face to face with four newly arriving German corps. Unaware of this massing of troops in front of him, and notwithstanding the lack of success attending his attacks, French continued to issue orders for attack on the 15th and subsequent days, insisting on even more ambitious advances eastward as part of an encircling movement pivoting on Lille and which was to extend far east of Ypres.

Confused actions took place on the fronts of all the British formations engaged; from time to time advances were effected and heavy losses were inflicted on the attacking Germans. Indeed, III Corps made a 3,000 yard advance beyond the Lys and reoccupied Armentières with minimal opposition on the 17th, after two days of little activity (and unnecessary local withdrawal) brought about by the corps commander's (Lt.-Gen. W.P.Pulteney) overly cautious approach. But by then further exploitation was impossible, and particularly the reoccupation of Lille, which the corps attacked in strength on the 18th, but which had been entrenched by the German *6th Army*, composed of the aforementioned newly arrived corps. In fact, the BEF was now heavily outnumbered both here and further north, to the east of Ypres where Sir Henry Rawlinson's IV Corps occupied the line. There was also severe pressure on the French, situated on the British left flank.

Nevertheless, Sir John French remained confident and urged IV Corps to move on and capture Menin on 19th October. However, it was on the defensive, under the weight of an attack (almost decisive in its effect) by the newly arrived German *4th Army*, eight fresh divisions strong. But such was French's optimism in the face of the, by now, full knowledge of the Germans' strength and dispositions (admitting that there were new corps in front of him he nevertheless dismissed them as 'Landwehr') that on 20th October he ordered I Corps (just arrived from the Aisne) to break out north-east of Ypres towards Bruges. Irrespective of his wishes, on that day II, III, the Cavalry Corps and 7th Division of IV Corps, (i.e. almost the entire fighting force of the BEF) were forced to entrench in the face of heavy German attacks by both *4th* and *6th Armies*.

The line was held, thanks to the shooting of the BEF and the exceptional targets presented to them by the attacking formations; nor should the efforts of the French be ignored, with their units sometimes mixed in with the British. The untrained new German troops had relied on enthusiasm rather than skill and their clumsy, massed ranks made easy targets for the British and French riflemen and machine-gunners, who inflicted immense casualties (the precise figures are unknown, but the Official History estimates that the new corps lost about half their infantry). Inroads, where made, were largely due to ad hoc penetrative tactics by small parties of Germans exploiting the many gaps or weak points in the British defensive line. Nevertheless, in many instances Allied (and particularly British) regiments took such heavy casualties that they were, on paper, wiped out; the German numerical and artillery superiority took their toll.

Time was not now on the Germans' side, for their opponents could only benefit by its passage to regroup, entrench and reinforce while they themselves were rapidly running short of trained officers and senior NCO's. Indeed, by this time the BEF was receiving a steady (though insufficient) flow of men from England, who were filtering through to the front line as the month drew to a close, although they continued to suffer from shelling and local attacks and were by no means secure. The Germans maintained the pressure on an almost daily basis, but nevertheless, a number of counter attacks were undertaken by the Allies. One German attack on the Messines-Wytschaete-St Yves Ridge, was witnessed by Lt. the Hon. Lionel Tennyson in 4th Division (III Corps):

> The next day, after a terrific shelling, which lasted from 8.15 a.m. to 3 p.m., the enemy attacked B and C Companies in force... The Germans advanced across the open in two solid lines with their officers in rear of the men. Our rifles and machine guns, however, simply mowed them down, and they broke and fled in all directions... Our casualties were

heavy, considering our small numbers, both in officers and men, but the Germans had left three hundred dead between their lines and ours.

As further protection the Belgians had now flooded the coastal region behind the Yser, masking the Allied left flank.

The Germans, meanwhile, massed a force of seven relatively fresh divisions, mainly drawn from the Aisne, under the command of General von Fabeck - and known as *Army Group Fabeck* - with which to renew their offensive on 31st October. Such was the confidence that this would succeed, that the Kaiser arrived at *4th Army* HQ in order to prepare for his triumphal entry into Ypres. The defence of the village of Wytschaete was, on this occasion, the task of General Gough's 2nd Cavalry Division, fighting dismounted in trenches which were often little more than shallow ditches. Br.-Gen. Philip Howell, at that time a major but commanding the 4th Hussars after the death of his colonel, described his regiment's part in this desperate fighting:

> This has been our biggest battle so far - at least it's all one continuous battle really, but the last few days have been more strenuous than usual. And for certain periods things looked rocky indeed. Now I think we're all right again... I don't know how much will ever be known, but for about 24 hours the regiment, quite alone, held the most important point in the line... Somehow the fighting round the south and east got divided into two sorts of groups... We filled the gap with a big reserve in rear. The fighting... became so serious that all the reserve got moved off north. And for 24 hours we filled the gap alone: and during that 24 hours new Germans came up in very great force and tried to rush the gap... I tried to blow up the canal bridge, but the wretched things wouldn't explode. So we then wired it up and hung on to the hill on one side of the bridge and road and to the edge of a wood on the other. All the week previously (when we'd been living in and holding the village on the hill) I'd thought that there might have to be a fight on this bridge, and so by good luck I'd had some very good trenches dug by the men who happened to be at any moment free. I've never seen or heard such a hell of shell fire as they poured upon our hill and wood! They must have had dozens of every kind of gun, both large and small. However, when the shell fire was hottest we hid behind the hill: and when the shell fire slackened to let their infantry come on to try to rush the bridge we popped up again and shot them down. All ranks behaved splendidly, for really it was a pretty severe trial. The maxim was about the middle of the little hill, in a rather prominent trench. K.C. was on the lookout there when a shell came right through his loophole and severely wounded him in half a dozen places. F— came down to report to me: I sent up the doctor, who reported that K.C. was so bad that he'd better not be moved. By this time there was another spell of heavy shelling, so I sent F— a written message to clear out of all the trenches and come

behind the hill. I enclose his reply - the last thing he ever wrote. Just afterwards in came another shell: blew F— literally to bits, destroyed my order, which therefore never got down to the troops: and broke poor little K.C.'s thigh. G— (attached to us from the Indian cavalry) called for volunteers and brought down K.C. still conscious and marvellously brave - just a mangled mess but quite quietly giving directions as to how he should be carried. He lived about an hour. Of poor F— they could find next to nothing. Meanwhile the shell fire got worse and two "Black Marias" dropped on to two trenches, each knocking out a dozen men - and then, and not till then, I realised that the order to withdraw had not got through. This time that we withdrew the German infantry came out pretty strong and the fire from the trenches (then reoccupied) was not enough to stop them, though a great many were knocked over. Just at that moment I got this other message from the Grenadiers about a mile away on our left. Being terrified that the bridge was going to be rushed I dashed off to seek for some Frenchmen who I knew were hiding in the wood near A. Found about 200 who at first refused to budge, for the shell fire was terrific; waving my arms, I yelled *"Allons, venons, nous avons cerné toute une compagnie d'allemands. Venez, venez nous aider les massacrer!"* - all in shocking French, but enough to be understood. That at once started them: and once started they behaved jolly well, and we drove the Germans back. Shortly after that, up galloped the 6th Cavalry Brigade - and that finished the show... I write now from a trench with the hell of a hallaballoo - the French passing through our weak little outpost line to attack a village called Messines in strength, with about 100 guns supporting them. Rather a fine sight, for they are getting on very well though very slowly. Their attacks seem generally to dwindle down to nothing, but this time they are driving on hard and I hope will get there. The German Emperor is said to be the other side of the hill: and Poincaré [the French President] was round the outposts on this side last night. To me it still seems more or less stalemate. I believe that the Germans have made tremendous efforts this last week: and have failed: and that they must be coming to the end of their offensive resources: and that we shall then be back more or less at the situation on the Aisne, both sides on the defensive, dug in and unable to move. It then becomes a mere question who can last out longest - a question of population and wealth and resources and temperament and grit.

While this action by the 4th Hussars and others retained the village, a large part of the Messines Ridge was lost and not retaken until June 1917.

Meanwhile at Gheluvelt, an important tactical location to the north, on a spur with good observation in all directions, the Germans actually broke through, but were driven out of the British lines in a famous local counter- attack in which the 2nd Worcesters played a decisive part, fighting at close quarters in the grounds of the Gheluvelt chateau.

The artillery, too, played an important part in supporting the infantry and dismounted cavalry. Often they fought alongside them and were in full view of the enemy and firing over 'open sights.' A subaltern of the Royal Field Artillery recorded the work and spectacular shooting of his battery in the battle:

> As I told you in my last scrawl we had one very exciting day, up with the 45th [battery], in cross support of the infantry. The infantry kept coming back in small parties, and we used to rally them on the guns and send them up again. We pumped a good deal of lead into German infantry advancing at about 600 yards range. We were in a wood to keep out of sight of aeroplanes, and could not have got out in a hurry, so we made a virtue of necessity and determined to stay there and chance it. The 54's were out in the open on our right and could have got away, but chose to see the thing through. The infantry managed to hang on all right, but we were prepared several times for shrapnel fire at 300 yards, should the Germans appear over the crest. As a matter of fact, the lowest range we touched was 1,200 yards, on an occasion when the Germans brought up a section of guns into a village in front of us. We were very fortunate to be where we were, as I do not think the infantry could have held on without us; there are limits to the power of endurance even of British infantry, and they had got hell that day.
>
> I watched a great shoot. A gunner subaltern had one gun on a long straight road, and a German gun came up behind a barricade on the same road, 900 yards away, and a duel ensued. The German got off the first two rounds, which went over; then our man put one of our new high explosive shells into the barricade and smashed it up, and followed it with a direct hit on the gun, bowling it completely over, and blowing the detachment up into the trees. [Major Francis Graham, DSO, MC]

Some ground had also been lost by the French between I Corps and the Cavalry Corps, and casualties were again heavy, but no breakthrough and rolling up of the line - which had been von Fabeck's intention - had been effected; the attack was broken off, to be renewed afresh on 11th November. Two divisions were sent in, straddling the Menin Road, to capture Ypres, with supporting attacks occurring elsewhere. At one point they broke through to the north of the road, and only artillery lay between them and the town, but they did not realise this. Hesitating, they were repulsed by a scratch force of whatever troops were available, including cooks and batmen. The fact that only these men were available to the British at this point, and only two divisions to the Germans in their main assault (as compared to the forces they employed on 21st October), indicates the scale of earlier losses on both sides. On 22nd November the battle was officially over and stalemate set in as the exhausted opponents strengthened their defensive lines.

The Ypres Salient had already gained a notoriety that it would never lose. And it was the graveyard of the Regular army; in those battalions which had landed in August and fought at Ypres against odds of four to seven to one, an average of one officer and thirty men remained.

Until the end of the year there was periodic fighting, but neither side undertook more than line-straightening and -strengthening operations. By then the BEF had taken almost 90,000 casualties (mainly in the first seven divisions, whose total effective strength on landing in France had been only 84,000) - three times their total battle casualties in the Boer War. When criticising the British armies on the Continent in later operations, it should be borne in mind that these losses in trained officers (and especially staff officers) and men, whose experience would have been invaluable to the New Armies being created in Britain, were crippling.

2

Feeling the Way:
Neuve Chapelle to Loos

The winter of 1914-15 was spent by both sides in improving their trench systems - when the weather permitted it - and in relatively small-scale fighting. However, the weather was at times so bad and trenches were so frequently flooded that many were abandoned and casualties owing to sickness became a significant drain on manpower, particularly in the 8th and 27th Divisions, most recently arrived at the Front and composed of units recalled from India (where they had been replaced by Territorials). The sudden and extreme change in climate was simply too much for many of these men to cope with. In fact, the decision to bring to Europe all those Regular troops who could be spared from garrison duty abroad had been made as early as 5th August 1914. In addition, 23 Territorial Force battalions had been sent to France in order to augment the Regular divisions already there (not until 28th February 1915 did the first complete Territorial division - the 46th - begin to arrive on the Continent). Consequently, by the end of 1914 the BEF had expanded to 11 infantry and five cavalry divisions. On Christmas Day of that year the orders were issued to reorganise it into two Armies: 1st, under Sir Douglas Haig, comprising I, IV and the Indian Corps; and 2nd, under Sir Horace Smith-Dorrien, comprising II and III Corps and the aforementioned 27th Division. The cavalry force of the BEF now consisted of the Cavalry Corps and the Indian Cavalry Corps.[1] In addition, recruiting in Britain and Ireland for the 'New Armies' called for by Lord Kitchener, the Secretary of State for War, had approached one million men by this time. However, the first of these were not ready to take the field until May 1915, and large numbers were not available until 1916.

Despite its reinforcements, the BEF remained at a disadvantage owing to lack of artillery pieces (and ammunition; late in 1914 and early in 1915, artillery pieces were often rationed to four rounds per day),

---

[1]   Indian troops arrived at Marseilles between 26th September and 14th October 1914.

machine-guns and specialised infantry weapons. While the Germans had gone to war equipped with hand grenades (known at the time as 'bombs'), rifle grenades, mortars, flares and the like, only a very few grenades were available to the British infantry, they began the war with their machine-guns far less efficiently organised than the Germans (giving rise to the erroneous conclusion that the latter had a higher number of guns per battalion), and the discrepancy in artillery was enormous. These problems persisted throughout 1915, although development of new weapons and expansion of the munitions industry were pushed constantly - and in the latter case, attended by a great deal of controversy. In the meantime, the troops in the trenches had to use improvised grenades (such as 'jam tin bombs', whose origin is self-explanatory) and mortars of varying degrees of lethality to friend and foe alike. Given this weakness on the British side and the Germans' concentration of their efforts on the Eastern Front, it is not surprising that the deadlock persisted.

Nevertheless, the offensive spirit continued to prevail in the BEF's high command and also in that of the French. The mainstay of military doctrine in both armies was a belief in the moral superiority of the offensive over the defensive, and that an attack pressed home in the correct spirit would overcome material deficiencies and the inherent advantages conferred by modern weapons on the defender. Despite the disastrous outcome of Plan XVII (with the loss of 300,000 casualties out of the 1,300,000 troops involved) as a result of such ideas, it was politically unthinkable for the French not to make the utmost efforts to expel the invader from their soil. And they expected the same commitment from the British, bringing strong pressure on a by no means reluctant Sir John French (and his political masters, by no means all of whom were convinced that a breakthrough was possible) to initiate a major attack as soon as possible in 1915. This was reinforced by the strategic need to draw German troops away from the Eastern Front, their High Command having decided to stay on the defensive in the west since they viewed operations against the Russians as having the greater chance of success. The outcome for the British was the offensive at Neuve Chapelle, intended as a prelude to the capture of Lille.

*   *   *

The attack at Neuve Chapelle took place on 10th March 1915. Sir John French's somewhat vague intention to stage an offensive, initially in conjunction with the French 10th Army to the south, was expressed to Douglas Haig on 15th February. Between then and the actual attack, however, the co-operation of the French was reduced only to artillery support, since Sir John had felt unable to accede to the demands of Joffre (the French Commander-in-Chief) for the British to take over more line (especially in the northern part of the Ypres Salient) as well as attacking. Consequently, the French felt that the British were not serious in the prosecution of the land war and so concentrated their troops on their own (unsuccessful) attacks to the south. The Neuve Chapelle offensive was thus rendered strategically pointless before it had begun, for the British were too weak to make a significant breach in the German lines.

In Haig's sector Neuve Chapelle village presented an attractive proposition for an attack, it being in a salient protruding from the German lines which allowed fire from the latter to enfilade part of the 1st Army defences. Conversely, this meant that a large concentration of fire could be directed onto the village from three sides, and furthermore, it was thought not to be strongly defended. However, the Germans had already begun to plan for defence in depth, with pillboxes to be manned by machine-gunners, 1,000 yards behind their front line; these were either overlooked or ignored by GHQ. Although such a line-straightening exercise was essentially a tactical operation, Haig was keen that 1st Army should undertake the BEF's first major attack, and so (lest 2nd Army be permitted to make the attack against the important Wytschaete-Messines Ridge to the north) he inflated the scope of the operation to include the capture of Aubers Ridge, between one and two miles beyond Neuve Chapelle, with a view to further operations to capture or at least threaten the German positions in the valuable mining areas around Lille. This won the approval of GHQ.

The operation was to be carried out by the Indian Corps, under Sir James Willcocks, and IV Corps, which was still commanded by Sir Henry Rawlinson. The latter was instructed to formulate a plan for the capture of Neuve Chapelle as early as 6th February; that this actually pre-dates Sir John French's discussions with General Joffre perhaps indicates the prevalence of the offensive spirit amongst senior officers. As the day of battle drew nearer, Haig intimated that he hoped for the breakthrough to Aubers Ridge. Despite this, Rawlinson at least was sceptical regarding the latter and certainly no serious consideration was

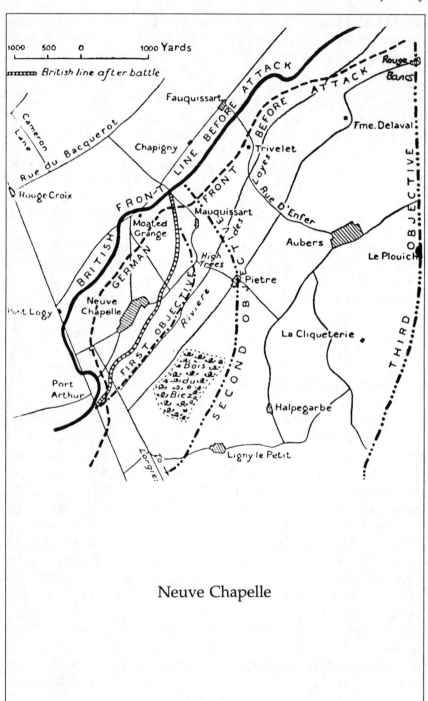

Neuve Chapelle

given to follow-up operations by either corps commander. However, Haig and his subordinates were in accord over tactics; the attack should consist of artillery preparation followed by a rapid storming of the enemy lines, although they differed as to the duration of the bombardment. It is interesting to see the way in which ideas had changed since Le Cateau; now the artillery was perceived as the vital factor in the attack, and the infantry was expected simply to walk through the shattered defences, with no great tactical finesse required on its part. Eventually a short but intense bombardment with a high concentration of artillery pieces was applied - one for every six yards of enemy trench.

Notwithstanding this firepower the defenders survived in large enough numbers to emerge from their dugouts and put up a stalwart defence. The attack was made on a three-brigade front, two from 8th Division (in IV Corps) and one from the Indian Corps. 23rd Brigade, in the centre, soon ran into difficulties owing to uncut wire and an active enemy; the howitzer batteries which had been assigned to this part of the line had only arrived the previous day, and there had not been time to register them properly. As a result they had simply missed the German front line, and for reasons unexplained, the 18-pounder batteries assigned solely to wire-cutting here also missed their targets. However, after suffering heavy casualties the 23rd Brigade took its objectives (as had the other two brigades in the attack). But it had been delayed by several hours, and in the meantime the successful 25th Brigade had been ordered to wait for it, even though it seemed that opposition to its front was negligible. Perhaps it was fortunate that this order was given, since (unknown to the British) two strongpoints had been occupied by the Germans during the bombardment and other reserves had been brought forward. Had an advance been attempted, it seems likely that these troops would have ensured that it was brought swiftly to a halt, for neither the tactics nor the technology for either infantry or artillery to deal with concrete pillboxes had been developed in 1915. Eventually, as a result of delays in communications between the two corps and their subordinate formations and because Willcocks refused to advance on any part of his line until all the first objectives had been taken, a push towards Aubers Ridge began at around 4p.m. (although even 23rd Brigade had reached its first objectives by 12.30!). This was a failure, taking place as it did in the face of an alerted enemy, in poor light, with no artillery support and over difficult ground.

Willcocks' delay exemplified a growing tendency towards rigid adherence to the original plan, with a consequent failure to grasp tactical opportunities as they arose, which was the consequence of dependence principally on the artillery plan. By the next day, the Germans had received substantial reinforcements and had considerably improved their defences. As a result, the renewed British attacks were doomed to failure, for not only did they face twice as many of the enemy as on the previous morning, but their artillery support was hopelessly ineffectual. Not only did mist hamper FOOs, but also the locations of the German defences were not definitely identified and so the guns were not necessarily even registered on the right targets. There were also undoubtedly lost opportunities brought about by lack of a clear objective beyond the first day's plan (notwithstanding Haig's ideas of a breakthrough) and by lack of co-ordination between regimental HQs and the higher command. CQMS A.S.Clapham of the HAC witnessed the failure of one assault:

> We were on higher ground than the attack and could see all that happened quite clearly. Bridges had been placed over the frontline trench, and I watched the attacking party cross. Our bombardment did not seem to have done much damage, for, immediately the attack started, the Hun trenches appeared to be full of men. One of them got out and sat on his parapet in spite of our rifle and machine-gun fire. The attack never had a chance. I watched the little khaki figures struggle on and fall one by one. Right in front of them was an officer with his cane. He strolled forward, and from time to time turned to wave on his men. He fell not far from the Hun wire, and not more than two or three others, at the outside, got so far. Very few indeed got back.
>
> It was a horrid thing to watch, and it was still more pitiful, the next day, to see the field in front dotted with the bodies of our men. The whole thing was so obviously useless and futile. There must have been at least twenty men in the German trench for every one who attacked.

On the third day of the offensive, some slight progress was made, and the British at least had the consolation of massacring a German counter-attacking force (assisted by a bombardment just as ineffectual as their own) in much the same way as they had suffered on the previous day. No further progress was made. Neuve Chapelle was taken, but nothing was gained in the grander scheme and the lesson of the operation, as absorbed by GHQ, was that given even more guns, a proper breakthrough could be achieved.

What they failed to appreciate was that the concealment of the guns before the attack, the care with which only a few were registered on their targets at a time, so that their overall numbers were not revealed to the enemy, and the use of spotter planes equipped with wireless to improve registration for the heavy artillery, all combined with the brevity of the bombardment to make the attack a surprise. This contributed greatly to its initial success. In addition, the ground over which the troops attacked had not been churned up as it would have been by a long bombardment, so that passage for the attacking troops was relatively easy. And their speed was increased by the use of rapidly moving columns of men without their packs, rather than the deliberate wave formations of fully laden men to be employed later. Another contributory factor was the willingness of commanders to employ the new technology available to them. Rudimentary aerial photography by the Royal Flying Corps had provided detailed maps of the enemy's defences, and had identified their gun positions. These became the object of careful counter-battery fire in the artillery fire plan. Furthermore, it was ensured that (for the first time) the types of gun available were given tasks commensurate with their capabilities, so that 18-pounder field guns used their shrapnel ammunition to cut wire, the heavier howitzers brought their plunging fire with high explosive ammunition to bear on German trenches and the heaviest guns were used to destroy strongpoints and for counter-battery work. Efforts were also made to secure the most up to date trench mortars, but these were to no avail and so the troops were equipped with models of poor quality.

The next attempt to take Aubers Ridge, on 9th May, was an equally, if not more unsuccessful attack, where the shortage of artillery ammunition was compounded by there being many duds amongst those shells available, by the wear on the guns rendering them inaccurate and by a change in the atmospheric conditions making their registration before the battle useless - not that most gunner officers yet perceived this problem. Furthermore, the Germans had learned from Neuve Chapelle. They had appreciated the effectiveness of shrapnel against barbed wire, and so placed much of the latter in trenches, which the 18-pounders, with their flat trajectory, were unable to reach except in the case of a direct hit.

Notwithstanding subsequent criticism, the BEF's commanders did try to learn from their mistakes (and it must be granted that these were often the product of inexperience in this new type of warfare). Both Neuve Chapelle and Aubers Ridge had suffered from being launched on relatively narrow fronts. In consequence, it was easy for German artillery and machine-gun fire on each flank of the attack to enfilade the assaulting troops, enhancing the defenders' natural advantages. While it was realized that a wider frontage of attack would reduce this problem, a heavier bombardment was also deemed necessary. This also served a political purpose, since the failures of Neuve Chapelle and Aubers Ridge were blamed by Sir John French and others solely on the ammunition shortage, avoiding any awkward questions regarding the artillery techniques themselves, or on the handling of the infantry.

*   *   *

The plan for the largely neglected battle of Festubert (15th-27th May) was therefore built upon the experiences of Neuve Chapelle and Aubers Ridge. Unlike the latter, when the two prongs of the attack had been 6,000 yards apart, at Festubert the gap was reduced to 600 yards, with the attacks taking place on frontages of 850 and 1,600 yards (to the north and south of the gap, respectively). Hence the total length of line assaulted was a continuous 3,050 yards, the intention being that the troops attacking would spread out to fill the gap on penetrating the German first line. This compared to 1,500 yards for the northern thrust and 2,400 for the southern at Aubers Ridge, with a much larger space between, which had effectively reduced them to completely separate assaults with little chance of linking up as planned. Furthermore, in order to achieve the convergence of the two prongs in the latter battle, the depth of penetration of the German defences had been planned as 3,000 yards, whereas at Festubert less ambitious objectives were set and an advance of 1,000 yards deemed sufficient. This battle, in addition to being the first British attack with limited objectives (and hence the first attritional attack), was also the first where a relatively lengthy preliminary bombardment was employed, in order that the effect of the shelling might be more closely observed. In places, the Germans were forced out of a line they had expended time and effort to construct, and into weaker positions. This afforded the British generals tantalising glimpses of the opportunities they might have been able to seize, given more reserves and artillery, in order to renew the assault promptly and employ these new tactics in order to secure a breakthrough. A follow-up to Festubert was the action of Givenchy on 15th and 16th June, which is noteworthy as the first occasion on which 4.5" howitzers were employed for wire-cutting.

* * *

Meanwhile, on 22nd April, the Germans had renewed their attack on Ypres. Using poison gas for the first time on the Western Front, in the northern part of the Salient, they overcame the French Colonial troops holding the line. Units of the BEF, rushed up in support, temporarily checked the attack. However, German persistence in the application of gas, and their substantial artillery support led to further loss of ground and heavy Allied casualties in unsuccessful counter-attacks, reliant as they were on rifles, in the absence of adequate numbers of guns, shells or protection against gas. Stephen Foot, an engineer officer, recalled the advice given as: 'urinate on a handkerchief is the only thing to do... if this is held over the mouth and nose the ammonia will neutralise the chlorine.'

One noteworthy repercussion of this fighting was the 'degumming' of Sir Horace Smith-Dorrien, under whose Army V Corps held much of the Salient (the rest being under French control). Given the cramped conditions of the latter and the high British losses, Smith-Dorrien felt that only operations conducted jointly with the French held out any hope of success. But they were not prepared to commit troops in numbers greater than had already failed in earlier attacks. Instead, therefore, on 27th April Smith-Dorrien advocated an organised withdrawal to a prepared position. This, he felt, would reduce the confusion of the situation, and by removing some troops from the Salient altogether, would reduce the density of targets available to the Germans. GHQ disagreed, though the events of the day bore Smith-Dorrien's view out. Nevertheless, before nightfall, he had effectively been relieved of the command of the troops in the Salient; the commander of V Corps, Sir Herbert Plumer was ordered to bypass his Army commander and report directly to GHQ. The bulk of Smith-Dorrien's troops having thus been removed from his control, and feeling that he had (unfairly) lost the confidence of Sir John French, he resigned as GOC 2nd Army on 6th May, to be superseded by Plumer. Ironically, the withdrawal Smith-Dorrien had proposed was carried out by his successor between 1st and 3rd May, before he had even resigned. This constitutes an outstanding early example of the sort of personality clash to which the officer corps of the British army was prone, and which continued throughout the war. Animosity between French and Smith-Dorrien (although they had been friends in the early years of the century) had grown since 1909, when the former had taken offence at ideas of Smith-Dorrien regarding the use of cavalry, which contradicted his own. And he had been most unhappy at Smith-Dorrien's appointment to command II Corps upon the death of its designated commander, soon after the latter's arrival in France in 1914. Indeed, French had favoured Plumer for the job even then.

Notwithstanding these high-level squabbles, the withdrawal proceeded smoothly. A soldier of the London Rifle Brigade participated in the operation:

> As a matter of fact, a retirement from the salient had been ordered two days ago, and some stages of it had been carried out already. It was all the more remarkable that these two German attacks did not upset all our plans. For the task was not an easy one to perform. All round the top of the "horseshoe" our troops were to withdraw silently that night, commencing at ten pm. In some places the front line was only a few yards from the enemy, so it can be imagined what caution was necessary. If he became aware of our intentions before the withdrawal were completed, the result would be disastrous. The contemplated retirement covered the whole front from Hill 60, which had been retaken by the Germans on 1st [May], to the Shell-trap Farm near Wieltje. Zonnebeke, Frezenberg, Fortuin, Zevenkote, Polygon Wood were all to be abandoned to the enemy, and I hope he enjoyed the smell. All the wounded were to be evacuated and all equipment taken away or destroyed.
>
> The retirement in certain places commenced at dusk, but we were not to leave our trench until the other troops to the north went - viz., 12.45 o'clock. The R.A.M.C. were soon on the scene with stretchers, and Pace, suffering intensely, was placed upon one; but he was, unhappily, not destined to live. Wood refused to wait a moment longer than necessary and disbelieved our promises that stretchers were coming. Two East Lancs, exceedingly happy and well fortified with rum, offered to lead him down, and it seemed best that he should hobble along lest through accident he should have to be left behind. The two Lancs were a bit too merry for my liking, and when they started to lead him east instead of west, I began to doubt their efficiency as guides. But Wood knew the way and guided them aright, and I saw him depart supported on either side, happy in the knowledge that he would soon receive proper attention. The blinded casualty was also removed, but he died in hospital.
>
> We next proceeded to collect all the rifles, boxes of ammunition, etc., and bury them near the road, the spots being duly noted by our colonel, ready for the return "push." Next came the dead bodies, which we determined to bury decently instead of abandoning them to the Germans. All this was done without arousing the enemy's suspicions, while in the "No Man's Land" between the two lines, our patrols were

active to keep him preoccupied. One of our men out on patrol, on seeing a German, shouted "Hands up." The German dropped his rifle, and our youth escorted his prisoner in proudly, the latter being over six feet high. One of our listening patrols, consisting of three men, was captured in a scrap, and we heard afterwards they were alive... When the hour came, we filed noiselessly out of the trench and moved off behind it towards Fortuin. Some of the East Lancs were left as a bluff, to fire their rifles occasionally and give the Germans the impression that the trench was held: these men were to follow at midnight. A flare or two went up and we flopped down, afraid that we should be discovered and that an attack or shelling might begin. We seemed to make too much noise; but the enemy gave no sign, and with great relief we filed on to the road, where, with as fleet a step as possible, we wended our way along past the field on the left where we had dug in upon the first night, past the graves of Pepper, Tucker and Woodward, past the spot where we had halted by the dead German on that memorable march up there. On and on we went, leaving behind us those hideous trenches, those thousands of bodies and those shell swept roads and fields. At Wieltje we passed ambulances, but a short while before we reached it we saw our new front line on either side of the road, manned by new troops, while barricades of barbed wire were ready to be stretched across the road when the last man had gone past. The enemy were not to realise our trick until the next day, and our trenches were shelled by them long after our departure. The regulars who had been left behind withdrew in safety and without the loss of a man - even the two Lancs who were the worse for rum "came to" the next morning and, finding their friends gone, managed to make their way down to their battalion again.

To the right and to the left the star-shells rose, marking the terrible salient as they had done nine days before, and for miles we plodded on without appearing to get far from the line. Through St. Jean we passed on, throwing nearly everything we possessed into the hedges and ditches, for we had hardly strength to carry ourselves along, let alone equipment and other encumbrances. Machine-gun ammunition, bandoliers of cartridges, entrenching-tools and other articles were cast aside, and the road was lined with the equipment of all those units that had passed before us. By daylight we were over the Canal, and feeling at last we were in comparative safety, lay down for a rest. [Rfmn. Aubrey Smith, MM]

After falling back towards Ypres the time came for counter-attacks and some ground was regained. Throughout May the battle continued with well prepared German attacks being countered by hastily organised and ill-supported counter-attacks. By the end of the month, both sides were short of ammunition (Sir John French had to bring offensive operations elsewhere to a close for this reason) and the troops on the ground were exhausted. Had the Germans not been concentrating on

the Eastern Front, the reserves they could have brought to bear might
well have given them a breakthrough. But the battle officially finished
on 25th May, with the French and British still in possession of the
Salient, though it was now reduced to such a size that German guns
could reach all parts of it, and their observers were well placed on the
low ridges overlooking it. Sporadic fighting continued in the Salient
throughout 1915 and 1916, until the Third Battle of Ypres expanded it
again. But events elsewhere meant that this was not to take place until
1917.

                    *   *   *

On 25th September 1915 the biggest British operation of the war thus
far was undertaken in the region of Loos, adjacent to the line held by
the French 10th Army. Since the operations earlier in the year the BEF
had been augmented by twelve divisions (both New Army and
Territorial Force) bringing its total strength to 28 divisions - or nearly
one million men - and the line they were responsible for extended
southwards from the Ypres Salient to Loos.

The new offensive took place at the insistence of General Joffre, who
was undertaking his own major operations in Artois and the
Champagne area and who required, rather than requested, British
co-operation. Initially, an attack was planned with the object of
capturing and holding the German front line,[2] using a three day
bombardment followed by an infantry assault, since the resources
available precluded any grander design. Sir John French agreed with
this and additionally urged that the objective should be attained
through the utmost reliance on artillery and on sparing use of infantry
in order to minimise casualties. At this stage of the plan it was, it
seems, universally agreed that any advance beyond the German front
line would be wholly dependent on French success in the south
presenting the opportunity to exploit German weakness in this sector.
However, Joffre applied pressure on Sir John to aim for a breakthrough,
and this was reinforced by the fears of the British government that the

---

2   It should be noted that the line referred to did not simply consist of one line of
       trenches, but was a complete system of front, reserve and support trenches, i.e.
       three in all. Hence, German defensive systems even in 1915 could well consist of
       nine or more lines of trenches. Later references in this book follow the same
       terminology.

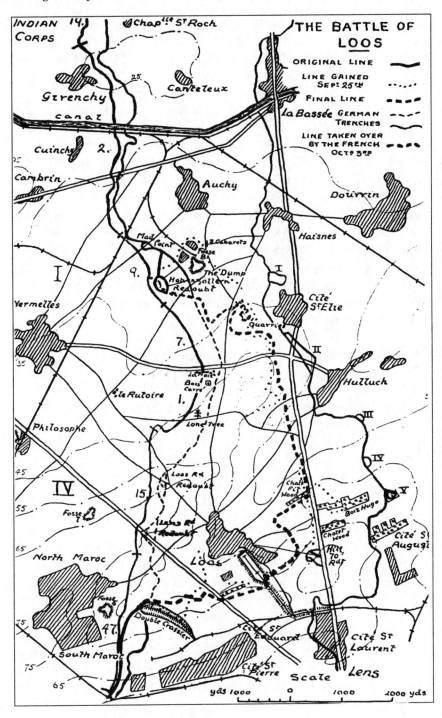

French or the Russians might make a separate peace. The position of the latter was at this time desperate, and so Lord Kitchener, the Minister of War, directed that a breakthrough should be the objective, in order to divert German reserves from the east and again to convince the French that Britain was serious in her commitment to the land war. The earlier caution was cast away as Sir John French urged the fullest possible support for the French plan despite the inevitability of heavy casualties. The objectives were expanded to include the towns of Loos and Hulluch, Hill 70 (beyond the former) and the German second line (an attack of some two miles in depth) and the front was elongated to include the line from La Bassée to Loos. As a result, I and IV Corps, which were to make the main attack (diversionary operations being undertaken by III and the Indian Corps), no longer had any reserves, since they now had to take part in the initial assault. Only the three divisions of GHQ reserve were now available, and Sir John insisted on keeping them under his direct command rather than that of the generals actually conducting the attack. Nevertheless, as the day of the offensive drew nearer, Haig, who as GOC 1st Army was in charge of the operation, became characteristically over-optimistic as his thoughts of tactical gain turned to visions of strategic success.

This optimism was ill-founded. The available artillery was fewer in number than had been mustered for Neuve Chapelle, and despite a four day bombardment (with no firing at night since the fall of shot could not be observed, and also giving the Germans the opportunity to repair some of the damage to their defences) compared to a hurricane 35 minutes at Neuve Chapelle, the concentration of fire per yard of enemy line was approximately one fifth of that brought to bear on the former occasion. And not only were there not enough artillery pieces to do their job effectively, but they were also hampered by the ground; parts of the German first and second lines could not be seen from the available OPs. Aeroplane spotting of targets was in its infancy and was in any case hampered during these operations by poor weather conditions. In addition, the 18-pounder guns employed for wire-cutting had to be placed a long way back, since behind the British front lay open country, with no cover for them. Consequently they fired at a longer range and so were less accurate. Furthermore, the German second line was completely out of their range, as well as being positioned on a reverse slope, thus making observation very difficult in the event of heavier pieces being used against it. Gas was to be used on the day of attack to make up for the artillery's deficiencies in its allotted role. It was calculated that in order to render the German gas masks ineffective they would need to be subjected to a gas presence for 40 minutes. But the cylinders[3] proved to expel gas for three minutes rather than the five that had been assumed, and because of the extension of the attacking front there were in any case too few to provide the required 40 minute release. Therefore, smoke was to be released too, alternately with the gas, in order that concealment could at least be provided for the attacking troops.

The final plan having been made, the bombardment commenced on the morning of 21st September. Philip Gibbs, the war correspondent, was impressed by the bombardment as he watched it, although some infantry officers he encountered were better informed:

> Storms of gun-fire broke loose from our batteries a week before the battle. It was our first demonstration of those stores of high-explosive shells which had been made by the speeding up of munition-work in England, and of a gun-power which had been growing steadily since the coming out of the New Army. The weather was heavy with mist and a drizzle of rain. Banks of smoke made a pall over all the arena of war, and it was stabbed and torn by the incessant flash of bursting shells. I stood on the slag heap, staring at this curtain of smoke, hour after hour, dazed by the tumult of noise and by that impenetrable veil which hid all human drama. There was no movement of men to be seen, no slaughter, no heroic episode - only through rifts in the smoke the blurred edges of slag heaps and pit-heads, and smoking ruins. German trenches were being battered in, German dugouts made into the tombs of living men, German bodies tossed up with earth and stones - all that was certain but invisible.
>
> "Very boring," said an officer by my side. "Not a damn thing to be seen."
>
> "Our men ought to have a walk-over," said an optimist. "Any living German must be a gibbering idiot with shell-shock."
>
> "I expect they're playing cards in their dugouts," said the officer who was bored. "Even high explosives don't go down very deep."

In fact, the bombardment was so puny by comparison to the French efforts to the south that it inspired confidence in few of the attackers. However, it brought an unintentional benefit in that the Germans

---

[3] Gas shells, a considerably more effective way of delivering the agent, had not yet been developed by the British.

assumed it to be a feint rather than the prelude to a full-scale assault, and so did nothing to counter it. As the shelling increased in ferocity on the third day, the troops also began to be more encouraged, and in fact it was surprisingly effective in some places. However, the gas attack having already lost most of its efficacy owing to insufficient quantity, it was rendered still less reliable by dint of the fact that it relied on wind of the right speed and direction - a factor over which the planners, of course, had no control. Nevertheless, all went well initially, as 5,500 cylinders of chlorine were placed in the front line ready for discharge.

In the south, where the 47th (London Territorial) Division were making the attack, the wire was cut and a rapid advance under the cover of smoke soon found them occupying the German front line; the gas had done little to influence operations in this sector. Pte. A.S.Dolden, 1st London Scottish, took part in the second wave of this attack, and it is clear from his account that even a successful advance was never free of difficulty:

> Our starting-off point was a reserve trench about a quarter of a mile behind the front line and in front of the town of Loos. At 7.30am we received the order to go 'Over the Top' and from then onwards it was like hell let loose. Bullets came flying round us from all directions, machine guns spat out their endless stream of lead, and shells came whizzing with a sickening screech, and burst with a deafening roar. Everywhere around us showers of earth from the enemy's barrage were thrown up.
>
> Our first casualty occurred when we had gone forward about ten yards and was a member of my Platoon. He fell shot through the arm. We had received strict instructions before going into action that no-one was to stop to attend to the wounded, as these were to be left for the stretcher bearers. It was very distressing to have to leave friends lying on the ground without being able to do something for them.
>
> We walked over the ground from the reserve trench to the front line. At our second halt Savereux fell at my side with a wound in the back from shrapnel. We next ran into enfilading fire, and the place become very warm for the enemy's machine-guns opened up on us. We had to advance over open country, and the Germans had us at their mercy. Just before the next halt, Walker, my own particular chum, fell shot through the left breast. He was next but one to me, but Fraser, who was next to him, was able to dress his wound before we received the order to go forward. It was hopeless, however, and he must have died soon after we left him. During the next rush we lost more men. There was a trench in front of us and we were ordered to get into it. I made a furious dive into the trench, and just missed empaling [sic] myself on the up-turned bayonet of a fellow who was sitting on the fire step. He was as much

surprised at my arrival as I was to see his up-turned bayonet point. We now had time to take a breather in this trench, for there seemed to be deadlock ahead of us. The company in front had reached the enemy's barbed wire, but, owing to their depleted numbers and also due to the strength of the rifle fire from the German front line, they were unable to advance any further; consequently they had to lie down in front of the wire and await events. Our Company was then told to try and work round and attack the German trench from the left flank. There was a shallow sap running a little way from the left of the trench in which we had halted, and this ran out to a tree which stood to the left of the enemy's line in No-Man's-Land. This tree had always been known amongst the troops as 'The Lone Tree'. Our object was to get across to this tree and to bomb down towards the centre of the enemy's lines, but owing to the rain that had fallen my bombs were useless as I was not able to light the fuse [Dolden was carrying 'cricket ball' bombs, which had to be lit with a match]. At this moment and in these circumstances I definitely felt that I was 'Cannon Fodder'. We left the trench and made towards the Lone Tree with the bombers in front.

We rushed across without sustaining any casualties but the trench was very shallow and only afforded shelter in places, so we had to lie as close to the ground as possible with our heads down, and then to leap up and rush forward in groups. We had not gone far when we came under the fire, not only of Germans, but also of our own men. In the excitement and confusion the regiment on our left flank mistook us for the enemy, and opened up on us with their machine guns. Holmes, the leading bomber, fell riddled with bullets through the head, and the rest of us had to crawl over his dead body. This was made more gruesome by the fact that we could see his brains spattered about him. We were all in a sorry plight because we could neither move forward nor backward, and we were being picked off one by one, for the little shelter that we had was not sufficient to protect us. Our numbers were too few to rush across the ground to the 'Lone Tree', for we would have been mown down before we got there. We were unable to get word back to our own men to stop firing, and so it seemed to be only a question of waiting for the end and trusting that it might be swift and painless. The tension was at its height when someone shouted 'Look at the Lone Tree; they are taking prisoners'. I looked up and to my utter astonishment and, needless to say, my unspeakable relief , saw the Germans coming out of the trenches with their hands up to give themselves up as prisoners. This turn in events had been brought about by the Black Watch who had broken through the enemy's left flank, and seeing that our boys were held up had turned to their right and so cut off the retreat of the Germans on our immediate front. The enemy, seeing kilts in front and behind them, evidently deemed it expedient to throw up the sponge, and so filed out of their trenches.

The attack on the left was undertaken by the 1st Division - Regulars -

who were not so fortunate. Here the gas blew back in their faces and several hundred casualties were caused by it. But the wire was partially cut and in some places the German first line was taken, although the attackers were severely hampered by casualties and by hanging flanks[4] where their comrades had been held up. The German second line proved well defended and intact and no further advance could be made without reinforcements. What reinforcements there were, however, were sent where the initial attack had been unsuccessful rather than to where a breakthrough was a real possibility. They faced the same uncut wire as the first waves and were similarly halted with heavy loss.

In the centre of the attack the 15th (Scottish) Division had the most difficult task: the taking of Loos and Hill 70, which lay beyond it. Here the wind was blowing in the right direction but not strongly, so that one brigade ran into its own gas, causing it to be held up and the brigades on its flanks to be enfiladed. Nevertheless, Loos and Hill 70 were captured. Beyond them lay the German second line - still intact and held in some strength. To take it without proper planning and support was an impossibility, but communication with HQs had broken down and bodies of troops pushed forward towards it only to be brought to a halt with heavy losses. For the time being, however, Hill 70 was held.

Meanwhile, congestion was building up behind the front as prisoners - where they had been taken - casualties, supplies of all sorts and reinforcements blocked up the roads. A chaplain who was present on the day found himself fully occupied:

> A few motor ambulances were trying to force their way through the mob in either direction. British guns had been brought up and were barking away in the fields on both sides, with an occasional German shell, of which no one took the slightest notice, exploding here and there. The only place that was absolutely deserted was the communication trench.
>
> Quality Street is not part of the Lens road, but runs parallel to it about 50 yards away for some 300 yards. Never in my life shall I forget the sight of that street - it was a sort of backwater from the traffic of the main road, given over entirely to the wounded.
>
> Two or three of the hundred and odd tiny houses were being used as dressing stations by the R.A.M.C. There was, I think, only one doctor in

---

4   That is, there were no friendly troops on each side of their position.

the whole street, a Canadian youth, who did not look above four and twenty and was considerably less, but no man worked harder that day than he did.

The cellars of several houses, more by force of circumstances than by design, were set apart as mortuaries, and every other house and cellar in the street was filled with wounded. In addition to this, the whole roadway from end to end was taken up with "lying cases" on stretchers, four deep across the road, waiting for ambulance cars to take them away. A car could only take four stretchers, and the main road was so congested with traffic that only now and then could a car be expected. One realised the grim truth that, while everything that could be done for the wounded was done, the first consideration was to win the battle, and for this purpose fresh troops and ammunition waggons full of shells and cartridges were of more importance than wounded men and had the monopoly of the road. ['E.A.F.']

On the second day of the battle, 26th September, two of the three reserve divisions (Guards, 21st and 24th) were committed to the battle. But by now the Germans had reinforced their second line - their new line of defence - with two divisions (so that more men were facing the assault than on the previous day), and these were attacked after a patently inadequate one hour's artillery preparation. Disastrously heavy losses (8,200 men in less than two hours) and the gaining of no ground were inevitable, and the Guards Division was sent in to contain the demoralised rout of the New Army troops of the 21st and 24th Divisions.

The offensive was renewed early in October and the last effort took place on the 13th with the attempted capture of Hulluch. The Germans were well prepared and the attack was a failure; after it the offensive was abandoned. Pte. Dolden again took part in the assault:

At 12.50pm our artillery began a concentrated bombardment on the enemy's trench immediately in front of us which, incidentally, advertised the fact that we were 'calling later'. This brought a furious reply from the Germans. Ten minutes later we all stood ready. Each of us had six smoke bombs; these we lit at intervals and threw out into 'No Man's Land'. The bombs emitted a cloud of dense smoke and a thick bank drifted towards the enemy lines. As soon as the Germans saw the smoke columns they let fly with every gun they had, and very soon there was a terrific barrage of heavy shells bursting over our trench. Heavy rifle fire came from the Germans in the trench in front of us, and so proved that the report of their weak numbers was untrue; in fact there were more in that German trench than in our own, and we found out later that they were all Prussian Guards, about the hardest nuts that we could have come up against. The machine gun fire was terrific, so much that we knew for certain that the little mystery cottage in the wood was bristling with them. True, our artillery got on to it, but this did not make the slightest impression, for the rate of intense machine gun fire never ceased all through the action.

Under cover of the smoke screen a party of bombers from the South Wales Borderers were sent along to reinforce us, and to hold the trench when we left to go into action. At 2pm we received the order to leave our haversacks and overcoats in the trench and to go 'over the top'. At the last moment the South Wales Borderers bombers were ordered to go over with us. This, however, they refused point blank to do, and allowed us to 'go over' alone.

The firing by this time had died down somewhat, for the Germans evidently thought that the smoke screen was merely bluff on our part.

We walked stealthily forward behind the smoke and, except for the occasional burst of rifle and machine gun fire, everything was going well till, unfortunately, a puff of wind blew away the smoke screen in front of us, and we were spotted by the enemy. Then everything seemed to happen at once.

Machine guns and rifles poured a deadly hail of lead into our small party. I had not gone far, when I was hit in the thigh by a bullet; it felt like a kick from a mule, and the force of the blow knocked me head over heels. I pulled myself together and then looked to my wound. Finding it only slight, the skin being merely grazed and slightly cut, I picked myself up and went forward. By this time I had lost touch with 'D' Company, so coming across 'A' Company who were going over on our right flank, I attached myself to them. On a closer inspection, I found that I had had a narrow escape. The bullet had hit the side of my water bottle, continued its course to the top, pierced the other side and, cut through five pleats of my kilt, grazed my side and eventually passed through the entrenching tool hanging on my belt at the back, and continued its career into space. The only injury that the bullet caused was the spilling of the water in the bottle - my sole supply for twenty four hours. In view of my escape I did not bother about this at the time, although later I regretted the loss bitterly when, in the heat of the battle, my parched throat ached longingly for a drink.

As soon as I joined 'A' Company, we could not move either way. The barbed wire in front was unbroken, so that we could not get through to the enemy trench, and a heavy barrage at the back of us prevented us from retiring. The heavy guns began to bombard us with shrapnel and, to put the finishing touch to our misery, our own guns, no doubt with a laudable intention of helping, began to shell the Germans in the trench in front of us. Unfortunately we were lying very close to the trench and a great number of the shells fell short and caught our own men. Shells were also falling on the Hulluch Road to our right, sending the granite sets skywards. These came down again in a shower, inflicting many wounds. Seeing that we could not go forward I dug myself in with a German entrenching tool handed to me by Sergeant-Major Morton, since my own had a bullet hole through it and so was useless for digging purposes. I lay flat on the ground and, with my right hand, burrowed away till I had raised sufficient earth to cover my head and shoulders. I also made a mound at the side to protect myself from the enfilading machine gun fire to which we were being subjected. On returning the entrenching tool to the Sergeant-major I found that he was dead. This was indeed a shock. Corporal Campbell was lying in front of me slightly to the right. He raised his head a few inches to fire his rifle. His body quivered and he sank back with a bullet through the temple. Very soon I was lying there with dead all round me. The Germans from the trench in front of us were firing very low in order to catch us as we were lying down, and I could hear the bullets rustling through the grass on each side of me. Behind I could hear the groans of the wounded. Every now and then one of them called out 'Mother, Mother', and at times 'Scottish'. Someone called out for morphia tablets, but of course there were none available. Our advance had been checked, and we survivors had to lie under hellish fire for four solid hours.

After the battle, the inevitable post-mortem took place. Intrigues against Sir John French had begun within days of the failure of the initial attack, the main charge against him, according to his detractors (prominent amongst whom were Haig and Rawlinson) being his mishandling of the reserves. Kitchener, Asquith (the Prime Minister), Lord Derby (the Director of Recruiting), the King and others were told that had the 21st and 24th Divisions been available on the first day of the attack, a great victory would have been won. This criticism ignored the fact that their positions were, at the nearest, five miles from the British front line, and so they could not possibly have reached the battlefield and been ready to attack before 2p.m. And by that time, German reinforcements had already come up to their second line, which had uncut wire, and there was no possibility of bringing British artillery up in time to be effective against it; as it was, communications between the artillery in its original positions and the FOOs had virtually collapsed. Nevertheless, French was replaced by Haig on 17th December; Haig's ally, Lt.-Gen. Sir William Robertson became Chief of the Imperial General Staff and General Sir Charles Monro took command of First Army to replace Haig. Rawlinson might have hoped to rise to higher command as a result of his intrigues. However, for the time being, all he was given was temporary command of First Army while Monro was in Egypt, in charge of the evacuation of the troops in the Dardanelles as the ill-fated Gallipoli campaign drew to a close.

3
The Big Battalions:
The First Day of the Somme
Offensive

1 915 had been a successful year for the Central Powers; the Allied offensives in the West had failed, the Dardanelles expedition had been a humiliating defeat, Serbia had been overrun and Russia had lost huge tracts of land, accompanied by tremendous losses in troops killed and captured. Although Italy had joined the Allies in May, she had soon proved to be more of a liability than an asset. Consequently, at the Chantilly Conference of 6-8th December, the Allied commanders decided to seize the initiative in 1916 and to prevent their opponents from concentrating their forces to make a breakthrough against any one of them by launching simultaneous offensives on the Eastern, Western and Italian Fronts.

As the senior partners on the Western Front, the French selected 30 miles between the Somme and Lassigny as the site of the attack in the west, and gained Haig's agreement to this on 29th December (the joint offensive had won approval in Whitehall the previous day). In fact, Haig preferred the idea of a summer offensive in Flanders, but in accordance with his ideas of the four stages of a battle[1] he appreciated that a wearing-down stage must take place before the main engagement, and this battle could as well be fought on the Somme as around Ypres. General Joffre wanted the attack to straddle the River Somme, with the British effort to the north of the latter, and to last - as the wearing-down fight - for three months before the main attack. After a number of discussions, Haig agreed to this, but with the amendment that the wearing-down fight was to last only for 10-15 days before the

---

1   These were enshrined in Field Service Regulations (1909) Part 1 (Operations) written by Haig, and were as follows: (1) The preparatory, or 'wearing-down' fight, designed to (2) pull in the enemy reserves and leading to (3) the decisive assault on the weakened enemy, which would lead in its turn to (4) the phase of exploitation.

main battle began.

While all this was going on, however, the Germans had made plans of their own. Although Germany was surviving a war on two fronts, it was a strain on her resources; this would obviously be alleviated if one or more of her enemies could be forced out of the war. Falkenhayn, the Chief of the General Staff, believed that France was more likely to be induced into requesting an armistice than Britain, for French dead already numbered over one million by the end of 1915. Further huge losses would surely prove unacceptable to public opinion. And to inflict them would not require a breakthrough; all that the Germans had to do was to attack a location which the French could not abandon, and the latter would pour men into its defence until their army was 'bled white.' After some consideration, the fortress town of Verdun was selected, since it was near the German railway communications (so a breakthrough, if it occurred, would reduce their vulnerability) and was in a sector of the line where the fighting could be restricted to a relatively narrow front, thus limiting its spread and so the potential for high German losses. The attack was launched on 21st February, and the fighting was ferocious. Although German losses were actually not much smaller than those of the French, the latter were great enough progressively to reduce the scale of French involvement in the Somme offensive, while making a major British attack all the more necessary in order to force the Germans to take men away from Verdun. Yet, curiously, it also had the effect of changing Haig's thinking about the Somme attack. He now felt that the wearing-down phase and that of drawing in the enemy's reserves had been attained by the Verdun offensive, and so were not required in his own.

In order to release French troops for Verdun, the BEF had to take over more of the line, which fell to 3rd Army (created in July 1915), and so 4th Army (created in February 1916, under Sir Henry Rawlinson) took responsibility for the Somme sector. The latter was quiet, and no reason justified its selection as the point of attack (had it been strategically significant, it is reasonable to assume that it would not have been a quiet sector), other than its being the area where the French and British armies joined. By early March, Rawlinson had begun detailed planning for his attack, and the massive administrative tasks required for it had also been set in motion. Accommodation for the troops (of whom there would be 500,000 by the time of the attack) and the livestock (100,000 horses, plus large numbers of mules and other animals), roads and railways, gun positions and ammunition dumps all had to be built. Trench systems had to be expanded to provide more forward observation posts, command centres, mines and assembly trenches. Medical equipment had to be stockpiled and dressing stations constructed; telephone cables were laid, 7,000 miles six feet underground (in order to prevent enemy shellfire from cutting them) and 43,000 miles overground. And fuel, oil and workshops for vehicles, and food and water (and water-piping and wells) for men and beasts had all to be provided as well. All this required an immense amount of labour, but only five labour battalions were available, and so the infantry themselves had to spend much of their time on this work - at the expense of their training. It also reflects the scale of the reinforcements received by the British forces in France. By the end of 1915 the latter consisted of 38 infantry divisions (organised into 11 corps) and five cavalry, totalling nearly one million men; a further 19 divisions (of which only ten had battle experience) had arrived by the middle of 1916. As much training as possible was carried out, however:

> Eventually it became known that our division would be in the attack and that the L.R.B. [London Rifle Brigade] would advance in waves, the details of which were worked out carefully. Indeed, it was clear that the battalion were to be well versed in what they were expected to accomplish, for, in course of time, shallow trenches were dug in neighbouring wheat-fields, modelled exactly upon the German defences as revealed by aeroplane photos. The British front line and the German first, second and third lines were indicated by little flags, and time and again the whistles would blow and the various waves, advancing through the corn, would take the successive lines of imaginary trenches. Every battalion that was attacking rehearsed on the same lines, each reproducing a different section of German fortifications, and making itself thoroughly conversant with them. If this went on throughout the attacking divisions, as I have no doubt it did, it says much for the care that was taken to make the advance a success. [Rfmn. Aubrey Smith]

Rawlinson knew that his men would be required to attack two German lines, each consisting of the usual arrangement of fire, support and reserve trenches, with concealed machine-gun positions and also with field guns placed between the first and second lines. Each was also defended by two belts of barbed wire 30 yards wide and 15 apart. In addition, a number of villages along the front had been heavily fortified and made into strongpoints, and the siting of the two lines on the ridges of the locality was such that in places machine-guns in the second could support those in the first line; direct artillery observation

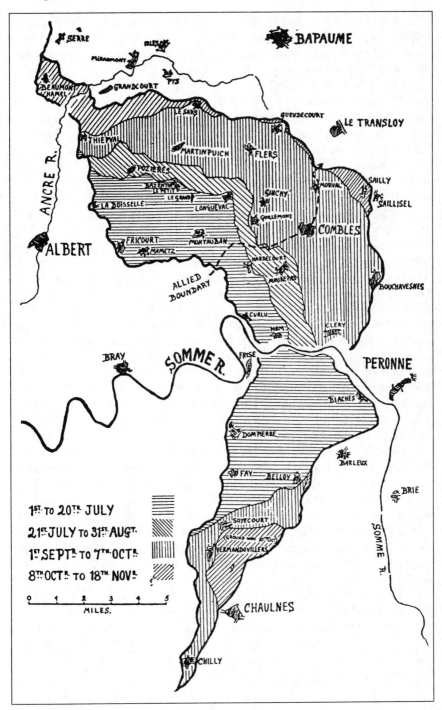

The Somme Battlefield

over the latter was possible from the former, and over the British lines (which were lower) from both. In other words, all approaches could be swept by rifle, machine-gun and artillery fire. Furthermore, the second line was on a reverse slope and lay beyond the range of those guns used for wire-cutting. However, initially he was in the rather curious position of not knowing quite what to do with the troops available to him once they had attacked; as noted above, no obvious strategic objectives lay behind the German position, and in any case, a breakthrough was not even on the agenda at this point. In a paper submitted to GHQ early in April, Rawlinson suggested a 'bite and hold' approach. In other words, he proposed that no breakthrough, or even the gain of as much ground as possible, should be attempted, but that tactically important points within the range of his artillery should be seized. The Germans would be forced to attempt their recapture, and so suffer heavy casualties. But whatever the ultimate objective, the main target had to be the system of ridges extending south-east from Thiepval to Guillemont, and the spurs near Gommecourt to the north and Montauban to the south. If these were taken, the positions on their flanks would be untenable, and given that no third line existed at this time (it was only in the early stages of construction) a breakthrough would more or less accidentally have occurred. However, this would necessitate an advance on a 26,000 yard frontage, and Rawlinson and his chief of staff, Montgomery, calculated that with the men available, they could only cover a 20,000 yard frontage. Consequently, the northern flank was trimmed and the northernmost objective made the village of Serre. But the problems of how to take the German positions and what to do with the ground taken still remained. The latter was answered by GHQ in response to the paper in April - Haig strongly favoured a breakthrough, and so Rawlinson was left in no doubt that he must plan for one. After further discussions, the plan the C-in-C more or less imposed on the 4th Army's commander was for the seizure of both the first and second lines on the northern part of the front, running from Serre to Pozières, and of the first line and ground extending up to two miles beyond it, on the rest of the front (i.e. a line running roughly from Contalmaison to Montauban). All this was to be achieved on the first day, with further advances subsequently. To assist in the exploitation phase, three cavalry divisions would be ready, under the command of Hubert Gough's newly formed Reserve Army.

To make the BEF's largest 'push' to date, 4th Army had five corps - from left to right as they held the line, VIII, X, III, XV and XIII (although when planning began, only VIII, X and XIII were available). These constituted 17 infantry divisions, of which the majority were

New Army and only four were Regular. Their weaponry was similar to that of the previous year, but some improvements had taken place. Light trench mortars were far more reliable and common with the issue of the Stokes mortar and grenades had become much safer (to the user) since the Mills bomb had become available to most battalions, although its weight meant that it could not be thrown far. More light machine-guns were available; the Lewis gun had come into service late in 1915, and it was planned that each battalion would have 16, although this target was not often reached, and some only had four. However, it was a short-range weapon, and in consequence could not always be used against heavy machine-guns; and in the event, because fewer were issued than had been hoped, some battalion COs held them back from the initial assault to support mopping up parties, so depriving the troops in the first wave of their firepower. In any case, while undoubtedly useful once in the German lines, none of these additions to the equipment of the infantry would help them get across No-Man's-Land. For that task, Rawlinson had to rely on the artillery.

The gunners' task was to neutralize or destroy the German defences and protect the infantry crossing No-Man's-Land. The BEF had far more heavy guns now than before; on 1st January 1915 it had had 36 batteries, but on 1st July 1916 it had 191. Of these, not all were used by 4th Army, but it had 200 6" or larger howitzers, and 1,500 guns in all. However, while far more artillery pieces were available than for previous offensives, the front of attack was also far wider, and once Haig had imposed the idea of a breakthrough on 4th Army, it was also deeper. Consequently the concentration of shellfire was far less than, for example, at Neuve Chapelle. Rawlinson therefore favoured a lengthy preliminary bombardment, which, while forfeiting any possibility of surprise, would at least (in his view) give time to deliver sufficient shells to cut the wire and destroy the enemy defences. In addition it provided more time for observation; heavy shells were still in limited supply, and hence were not to be wasted. After a struggle, he managed to convince Haig of the validity of these arguments, despite the latter's favouring a brief, hurricane bombardment; as a recent book[2] has observed, with the relatively slender resources available, only a stiff breeze would have resulted had Haig prevailed. A five-day

---

2   *Command on the Western Front*; see bibliography.

bombardment was agreed upon, to begin on 24th June, though because adverse weather hampered observation it was extended and the attack was scheduled for 7.30a.m. on 1st July.

The result of all this careful and lengthy planning and preparation was that 4th Army (and VII Corps of 3rd, carrying out a diversionary attack to the north) suffered the worst casualties in a single day in British military history; 19,240 dead and 38,230 wounded. A comrade of Aubrey Smith described what had happened in the 3rd Army diversionary attack at Gommecourt; many of the 4th Army assaults failed in the same way, although German artillery fire was worse in this sector than in any other:

> What had caused the failure then? Fulkes told me what he knew. The bombardment had played havoc with the German lines, and, before attacking, our men had stood up and watched the wood being pulverised by our heavy shells, a sight which roused them to enthusiasm in spite of the return fire they received from the German guns. The enemy put down a protective barrage, but our attack started off in great style, under cover of numerous smoke bombs. The ground to be covered was from two to three hundred yards across, and the German machine-guns had a good field of fire before our boys reached their first trench. Many men fell from machine-gun bullets and others from shells, which the Germans were sprinkling about No Man's Land, but the waves reached the front line where there was bomb-fighting with the garrison; in the meantime the British were continuing to shell the wood itself. The front trench seemed to be smashed to atoms so the men passed on to the second objective, then to the third line, where Gommecourt was almost within their reach. Here they had to wait for reinforcements, reduced in numbers but quite full of fight. Time went on, however, and no fresh waves appeared, while on the other hand aggressive parties of Germans were bombing their way up communication trenches from behind them. They had been lurking in huge dug-outs under the ground which had survived the bombardment, and were now disgorging bombers by the hundred. The first and second lines had not been "cleaned out" by the captors who, it should be said, had never been led to anticipate such huge underground caverns, and therefore took less notice of their unpretentious openings than they would otherwise have done. The German bombers swarmed all round the advanced elements, who soon began to realise that they were surrounded and trapped as the hours went by. There was nothing to do but use their bombs sparingly and wait for reinforcements.

> To the intense surprise of all, the reinforcements never came through, though they started to time from the 56th Division trenches. The German artillery barrage, strong at the outset, had now increased to such a curtain of fire that it was almost impossible to pass through

unscathed. Here it is necessary to state a fact which was not known to Fulkes at that time. The 46th Division on our left, north of Gommecourt, only reached the front line and got turned out of it again; the defeat was swift and took place while our division was still actually advancing, thus enabling German guns behind the Gommecourt salient to turn their full fury on to our divisional front. German machine-gunners and bombers, too, satisfied that the attack was definitely strangled north of the wood came to the assistance of the enemy in our quarter. The bombardment from our side had now lifted on to Gommecourt, consequently the Germans mounted their machine-guns on the parapets with a clear vision and perfect targets, while the wall of shells, cutting off the attackers from further supports, continued hour after hour. Again and again men started off carrying ammunition and bombs - the latter being a vital means of self-preservation in the captured trenches - but they were all annihilated. Prisoners with escorts started back from the German lines, but did not survive the barrage.

The small bodies of our infantry who were holding on, having run out of bombs, used German grenades for a time until these were exhausted. Presently the more advanced elements had to abandon their wounded and make a bolt to the rear. But the Germans were becoming more daring, knowing that our men were trapped, and they mounted their machine-guns in the open while their bombers, drawing upon inexhaustible supplies, made it impossible for us to remain in their trenches. The run for life had to be attempted. From shell-hole to shell-hole the survivors darted, sniped at by Germans whenever they appeared, bombed when they remained in hiding. Third, second and, finally, first objectives had to be abandoned, leaving dead, wounded, equipment and tools behind, while the race across the two hundred yards of No Man's Land faced every man who lived until the afternoon. Through the intense artillery barrage and under heavy machine-gun fire men dropped right and left, until the ground between the trenches was an awful scene of carnage. The attack was over, and the best part of several battalions lay before our lines in this sector alone. (Rfmn. Aubrey Smith, MM)

As at Gommecourt, in many places footholds had been gained in the German lines, but hostile artillery fire made it impossible for these men to be reinforced as they were assailed by the numerous Germans who had survived the 1,600,000-shell British bombardment, and so VIII, X and III Corps failed to make any lasting advance. On the southern flank, XV and XIII Corps achieved far more, two divisions (18th and 30th) of the latter even gaining all their objectives (including Montauban), though with casualties scarcely lighter than the other corps. This is in part because the French 6th Army was launching its attack on XIII Corps' right, and so its artillery also supported the British. It is noteworthy that, with a more than tenfold superiority in numbers of artillery pieces over the Germans they were attacking, the French managed to take all their objectives, and even in places to advance further, with relatively light casualties. The 21st Brigade took part in 30th Division's attack. The commander of its machine-gun company described it; the contrast with 56th Division's is remarkable:

> At 7 the intense bombardment began, and our machine-guns opened again on the German communication trenches. The mist was clearing off. The officers had joined their sections, and I went forward with two orderlies to the H.Q. of the supporting battalion, which were to be my H.Q. too.

> There was a wonderful air of cheery expectancy over the troops. They were in the highest spirits, and full of confidence. I have never known quite the same universal feeling of cheerful eagerness.

> The moment came, and they were all walking over the top, as steadily as on parade, the tin discs on their backs (to show the guns where they were) glittering in the sun... Very soon German prisoners began to come back, and we could see our leading lines topping the German support lines.

> Our Brigade was to take and hold the trenches and redoubt opposite us, and then another Brigade [90th] was to go through, half left, and take an important village (all this was accomplished up to time, though the fact that the Division on our left [18th] was held up for a bit hampered us a good deal)...

> Somewhere about 10 o'clock the Colonel of the supporting battalion and myself moved forward... We went up to our front line and on to and across the "racecourse" [No-Man's-Land]... I realized that two lines of Pioneers were steadily digging away at two communication trenches across the "racecourse"; that they had been there for some time, and would be for many hours more... They lost about 25 per cent, I believe, but made two fine trenches...

> All had gone well: the guns had reached their objectives, luckily with small loss. The *nettoyeurs* (people who clean out the deep dug-outs - a most important job, as otherwise the Boche emerges and takes you in rear) had done their job well; and in front the Redoubt was in our hands.

> Before starting... I had watched the other Brigade going for the village [Montauban], which lay on the top of a rise across a valley. They had little opposition getting into it, though they were badly shelled there afterwards... but the cost of the advance was not heavy. [Major H.F.Bidder]

The reasons for the varying fortunes of the British corps are numerous.

The crux of the whole matter is that the formations subordinate to 4th Army operated in a tactical vacuum. Sir Douglas Haig felt that it was for the commander on the spot to decide what infantry and artillery tactics to employ, but unfortunately, Sir Henry Rawlinson made no attempt to impose a consistent system for either upon his corps and divisions, although in fairness, 4th Army issued a number of reasonably helpful pamphlets on such matters. In the realm, firstly, of infantry tactics, this had a number of effects. The traditional vision of heavily-laden men labouring across No-Man's-Land at walking pace (and under orders to go no faster) is inaccurate. Depending on the nature of the ground, the presence or absence of substantial German strongpoints, or simply a given commander's faith (which generally was not great) in the initiative and training of his New Army troops, the attack formations could vary from division to division or even between battalions within a given division. Some were permitted, as in previous battles, to advance in small, fast moving columns; others had waves imposed on them. In the latter cases, it is often recorded that in any case, once they were subjected to the Germans' machine gun fire, the attackers quickly, and from necessity, abandoned their waves and packs and advanced across No-Man's-Land from shell-hole to shell-hole, in small groups. In the same way, the use of smoke to conceal them also varied, even though Rawlinson was known to favour its employment, having found it effective at Loos; those doing so generally suffered fewer casualties initially. Aubrey Smith's account (while relating to 3rd Army) given above shows its effect - his 56th Division was largely successful in entering the German positions, whereas the neighbouring 46th was delayed by various obstacles and so much of its smoke cover had dispersed by the tine it was half-way across No-Man's-Land, and it suffered accordingly. In one particular instance, a corps commander's decision to deviate from the arrangements elsewhere was disastrous. Lt.-Gen. Sir Aylmer Hunter-Weston,[3] commanding VIII Corps, had in place under the German lines a large mine (i.e. an underground chamber or chambers, crammed with high explosive). This he decided to blow at 7.20, ten minutes before the main attack went in. As a result, the Germans were thoroughly alerted, and as the attacking divisions formed up in

---

3   Hunter-Weston, who had so adroitly slipped his 11th Brigade across the Aisne in 1914, had in the meantime suffered severe sunstroke at Gallipoli, from which his staff felt he had never fully recovered. After 1st July 1916, he was not involved in a major attack until the Final Advance in 1918.

No-Man's-Land, they were met with intense fire. Successes were fewest and losses greatest for VIII Corps.

However, the most sophisticated infantry tactics then devised would not have helped the attackers, for the simple fact was that there was not enough artillery (or reliable enough ammunition - many shells were duds) to cut all the German wire, kill all the defenders (many of whom were concealed in deep dugouts) and suppress their artillery. And even had more been available, British gunnery was not in July 1916 technically capable of sufficiently accurate fire to do the job, though matters had in some respects improved since Loos. Accurate meteorological information was now being sent from GHQ to the guns (though insufficiently often and lacking in detail) and artillery co-operation with aircraft was much better. But simply locating a target was difficult, since the area behind the German lines could hardly be mapped on the ground, and there were problems in the transposition of aerial photographs on to maps. Although other techniques were being developed to locate German batteries, they were not in widespread use on the Somme. And in any case, the amount of counter-battery work undertaken varied from corps to corps, owing to 4th Army's lack of direction. At least, however, its importance had been realised since Loos. Reliance on FOOs remained the norm; Lt.Col. N.Fraser-Tytler described the problems he faced:

> 26th [June]... We got in a lot of heavy shooting during the morning, including one concentrated strafe on German's Wood. It was certainly the noisiest day since the beginning of the bombardment. Every order to the guns has to be written on slips of paper, it being absolutely impossible to make anyone hear the spoken word. The Hun continued to reply hotly; until then he had been ominously quiet, and what with frequent prematures [i.e. shells bursting in or near the guns firing them; another hazard of faulty ammunition] the valley became pretty unhealthy.

> In the afternoon I went down to the front line with Wilson in order to engage a portion of our zone which was difficult to see from our O.P. However, we had not been shooting long before some of our very heavy Howitzers started a combined shoot on the Hun front line. It was a wonderful sight to see these huge shells bursting 300 yards in front of us, with detonations like earthquakes and smoke of every colour, black, white, grey, yellow and brown, rising often hundreds of feet in the air. However marvellous as a spectacle, this show did not conduce to accurate observation of our own small stuff, but by firing salvoes I was occasionally able to pick out my own bursts.

The effects of a lengthy period of firing on the guns and howitzers themselves had not been appreciated either. Prolonged firing reduced accuracy through damage to the bore; but it also lengthened range, by slightly turning the nose of the piece upwards. In the case of the 18-pounders firing shrapnel, buffer springs became worn, so that after the buffers had absorbed the recoil, they did not return the barrel to the same position every time.

The question now arises as to how, under such adverse conditions, did XV and XIII Corps achieve their successes? Firstly, their artillery fired creeping barrages, rather than bombardments which simply jumped from one trench line to the next. Some other corps had also done this, but XV and XIII Corps' were slower and more accurate, and the infantry, who had lain out in No-Man's-Land before the attack, were able to follow more closely and get into the German defences before their occupiers were ready to receive them. In addition, more troops were assigned to deal with Germans concealed in dugouts than elsewhere. And finally, the German artillery was far weaker than on other corps' fronts. In fact, a considerable opportunity was lost here to exploit this success and go on to capture positions which would later consume far more effort and losses. But the problems of communication on Great War battlefields meant that Rawlinson was not apprised of the situation until too late, and corps reserves had in any case been earmarked for later operations; the plan's rigidity stifled initiative. But at least the creeping barrage (first used in a primitive form at Loos) had demonstrated its worth; this line of bursting shells, moving forwards at walking pace, was to become a crucial feature of many successful attacks in the future.

4
Battles Lost and Won: The Somme, July to November 1916

It may seem disproportionate to have devoted the whole of the last chapter to only one day and the preparations beforehand, while this deals with the whole of the subsequent four months. But 1st July 1916 was the first day of large-scale operations for the BEF, and hence a crucial turning point in its experience. This chapter deals with the way in which the lessons taught on 1st July were slowly applied and refined in later fighting on the Somme.

By 3rd July it had become clear to both Haig and Rawlinson that VIII and X Corps were in no state to renew the offensive without reinforcement by fresh divisions. Furthermore, there was insufficient artillery ammunition to permit such a renewal along all of the original front of attack. Therefore, to avoid delay, III, XV and XIII Corps were ordered to continue operations with a view to securing various preliminary objectives, such as La Boiselle, Contalmaison and Mametz and Bernafay Woods before making an attack on the German second line in the southern sector. Casualties were heavy, and not all objectives were taken by the time of the big attack on the second line on 14th July. Once again, Rawlinson had not exercised his authority as army commander to ensure co-ordination between the corps. Some attacks were made with only a fraction of the artillery resources available, as on 7th July, when divisions from III and XV Corps were attacking; no contribution was made by XIII Corps gunners, even though their infantry were not involved. However, enough ground was gained to provide a reasonable start line for the next 'push.'

Little effort seems at this point to have been made to assess whether the available artillery resources were sufficient. Fortunately, they were, since the front of attack was 6,000 yards wide (rather than 20,000) with far fewer supporting trenches behind, and the number of guns and howitzers was two-thirds of that used on 1st July. Consequently, the intensity of fire possible was far greater than on the latter date. While creeping barrages were not uniformly applied, or counter-battery work closely attended to, the weight of shell made up for such shortcomings in the plan. This was assisted by the realisation that the final, intense bombardment should not be 30 minutes long, as on 1st July, for this had thoroughly warned the defenders (and their artillery) that the attack was imminent. Instead, it was to begin only five minutes before the infantry moved forward. Where a creeping barrage was fired, in order to prevent premature detonations of shells owing to their hitting trees or buildings, only high explosive shells with delay fuses were fired by the 18-pounder guns and 4.5" howitzers employed. On 1st July only shrapnel had been fired, but from 14th July onwards, shrapnel-only creeping barrages were a rarity. The more widespread adoption of the creeping barrage also represented a radical change in the BEF's thinking; the purpose of the artillery on the day of attack was not to destroy enemy positions, but to neutralise them, by inducing the defenders to stay under cover until the assaulting troops got there. Another novel feature was that because the German line was 1,500 yards away, Rawlinson proposed that the attacking troops form up in No-Man's-Land under cover of darkness, and make the assault at dawn. While Haig was initially highly sceptical of this idea, Rawlinson and two of his corps commanders (Horne of XV and Congreve of XIII Corps) eventually managed to win his agreement, with various provisos of which the most important - to Haig's credit - was that Rawlinson pay more attention to counter-battery work. Should a breakthrough be achieved, the 2nd Indian Cavalry Division would exploit the success by moving forward to take High Wood and the German switch line (part of the third) east and west of it, and other cavalry divisions were to be employed elsewhere. If XV Corps moved up to this position, the cavalry was expected to advance still further. How it was expected to cover the cratered and trench-strewn ground between the old British and new German front lines, seems not to have been considered. To expect it to go thousands of yards further still seems utterly unrealistic. An artillery officer who was in action that day wrote:

> The "intense" bombardment began at 3.20 a.m.; the infantry attack was launched five minutes later. Even to attempt to describe this bombardment is beyond me. All that can be said is that there was such a *hell* of noise that it was quite impossible to give any orders to the guns except by sending subalterns from the telephone dug-out to shout in the

ear of each sergeant in turn. The battery (in company with perhaps a hundred others) barraged steadily, "lifting" [i.e. creeping] fifty yards at a time from 3.25 till 7.15 a.m., by which time some 900 rounds had been expended and the paint on the guns was blistering from the heat. We gathered...that the attack had been very successful.

At midday cavalry moved up past us and affairs began to look really promising. Slept from 3 to 5 p.m., then got orders to reconnoitre an advanced position in front of Acid Drop Copse... Chose a position, but could see that if and when we do occupy it, it is not going to be a health resort. And, owing to the appalling state of the ground, it will take some driving to get there.

July 15. - Attack continued. By 10.30 a.m. our guns had reached extreme range and we were forced to stop. (We started at 2700 [yards range] in this position.) News very good: enemy much demoralised and surrendering freely. Practically no hostile shelling round us now... In the afternoon switched to the left, where we are apparently still held up, and fired occasional salvos on Martinpuich. Ditto all night. [Jeffrey E.Jeffrey, RA]

As this anecdote indicates, thanks to the power of the artillery, almost all objectives were taken and Rawlinson ordered the cavalry forward. They immediately encountered problems owing to unbridged trenches and slippery ground as a result of recent rain. Consequently, a long delay in their appearance was inevitable, and once Rawlinson had realised this, he ordered XV Corps to take High Wood. However, German reserves arrived far more quickly than had been expected, and prevented any further advance until evening. The delay occasioned by Rawlinson waiting for the cavalry before ordering XV Corps forward to the empty High Wood, has often been viewed as a great lost opportunity, but in fact the German reserves lay between XV Corps and the wood, and in any case it was not free of German troops. As it was, by nightfall British troops were entrenched half way across it, and 6,000 yards of the German second line, running between Longueval and Bazentin-le-Petit had been seized.

Curiously, Rawlinson did not seem to learn from the artillery success on 14th July. The next weeks were spent largely in a series of relatively small, uncoordinated attacks on narrow frontages and often with inadequate artillery support (see above; Jeffrey's battery soon found that the infantry had advanced beyond their effective range). The latter meant that the defenders and their artillery were unsuppressed, and the former, that the attackers could be enfiladed by neighbouring German troops who were not under attack, and all their artillery in the area could be concentrated on the threatened area. This grim crawl forward, often characterised by bitter fighting in woods, had, at first, only the virtue that the Germans were taking heavy losses, for they were ordered to retake all captured positions and so squandered their men in counter-attacks, adding to the heavy toll of casualties already inflicted by the British artillery. However, an innovation guaranteed that the British would lose more heavily than their opponents if they were not given substantial artillery support. Realising that, were the latter available, they would be destroyed in their trenches, German machine-gunners started to establish themselves in shell-holes behind their front line in order to escape the barrage. The front line was held only lightly and the defenders deployed in depth, ready to counter-attack. Consequently, the artillery's job was made far harder by the necessity of undertaking area bombardments, rather than simply shelling the German trenches. However, in this period (up to 15th September) the British advanced about 1,000 yards over a five-mile front. This was a smaller gain of ground than on 1st July, and casualties were about 30% higher than on that day, but the start positions (other than High Wood) for the next big attack had been reached. To the south, the French had also advanced (a number of 4th Army's operations, such as the capture of Guillemont, had been in their support) and were also ready for the attack of 15th September.

While 4th Army was to do the bulk of the fighting on that date, Reserve Army had a subsidiary role. It had taken over the northern sector of the old front line, from Hébuterne to the Albert-Bapaume road, soon after 1st July. From late that month, it had been moving forwards gradually, just north of the road, capturing a number of strongpoints, and with them, positions from which to dominate Thiepval. In particular, I Anzac Corps had distinguished itself in the fighting for Pozières.

The plan for 15th September had the aim of capturing the old German third line, and the two new lines subsequently constructed behind it. While none of these was as strong as the original trench systems, they still constituted a formidable obstacle. Discussions between Rawlinson and Haig followed a familiar pattern, the former wanting to take the three lines in a three stages, with short breaks between them in order to reorganise the infantry and bring artillery forward, and the latter wishing to rush all three in one operation and send in the cavalry to exploit the breakthrough. They would form a defensive flank on the right and the infantry would roll the German lines up to the north. This ignored the difficulties of getting the cavalry ten miles through trench systems and ground churned up by shellfire. Furthermore, the new third line was out of artillery range, and the problems of moving forward over broken ground in order to destroy it would be far greater for guns even than for cavalry. In addition, the technology for gunners to register quickly on new targets had not been developed. Needless to say, Rawlinson capitulated; an unfortunate aspect of the decision-making process in the army as a whole was that subordinate officers were not expected to argue with their superiors, and after his conduct of operations since 14th July, Rawlinson was in any case not in good odour with the C-in-C.

Crucially, as on 1st July, the more ambitious plan considerably increased the size of the position to be shelled and so reduced the intensity of fire; on 15th September it was less than half that on 14th July. This was exacerbated by the new German defensive tactics. However, a new weapon was to be employed for the first time - the tank.

When considering the role of the tank in the First World War, it is necessary to remember that those employed were not of the same breed which proved so effective in the Second. The Mark I had a maximum speed of two miles per hour over broken ground, was very vulnerable to artillery fire, prone to mechanical breakdown and arduous in the extreme to operate. Its engine was mounted inside the same compartment as the crew (eight men) which sent the temperature soaring and added carbon monoxide to the stale air, not to mention making it almost impossible to move around. Views of the outside were provided by peering through glass prisms, which had the habit of sending splinters into the viewers' eyes when hit by bullets. And just rifle or machine-gun fire could lead to an uncomfortable phenomenon called 'metal splash,' where the bullets' impact sent white-hot flakes of metal flying off the inside of the armour. Armament consisted of either two six-pounder naval guns (mounted in sponsons on the sides of the tank) and four machine-guns in the 'male' or six machine-guns only in the 'female;' these weapons also made their contribution to the fumes inside the vehicle.

One myth of the Great War is that all senior commanders were resistant to innovation. Given their ready acceptance of, for example, trench mortars, gas, and new and technically sophisticated artillery techniques, this view would seem to be inaccurate. The same was true for tanks. Once they had actually been produced and demonstrated to Haig and Rawlinson, they were very keen to use the new vehicles. Indeed, another criticism of Haig in particular is that he was too keen, and that the surprise should only have been sprung on the Germans once more tanks were available. This rather assumes that they were to fight on their own, ignoring the fact that the artillery was still vital to any attack, and it would not have the ability properly to complement the tanks for another year. Sir Douglas Haig did not have the ability to see into the future, and no general worth his salt would indefinitely postpone the use of a promising new weapon.

The tanks were to be used in small groups to help the infantry take German strongpoints, and especially the village of Flers. However, it was assumed that they would be faster than the infantry, which led to a risk of their running into the creeping barrage (by now GHQ was stressing the latter's importance to all attacking divisions). Consequently, Rawlinson ordered that 100-yard wide gaps be left in it, down which the tanks would advance. This was rather strange thinking on his part, since those points to be taken by tanks (and supporting infantry) were necessarily the best-fortified in the German lines; he was nevertheless denying the attackers artillery support, apart from the three-day preliminary bombardment. The creeping barrage was in two respects an improvement on previous attempts; it was slower, so that the infantry could keep up with it over broken ground, and it was denser, in an attempt to deal with German troops sheltering in shell-holes.

The Canadian Corps of the Reserve Army was on the left of the attack, with its objective the village of Courcelette, and 4th Army's III, XV and XIV Corps (from left to right) were to take the German positions extending from Courcelette round to Morval and Lesboeufs - a distance of about three and a half miles. To the right of XIV Corps, the French were also to attack. Zero hour was 6.20a.m., and Rawlinson expected all objectives to be captured by noon, leaving plenty of daylight for the cavalry to come up. Apart from the tanks, no tactical innovations were made, but, as noted above, the barrage was improved and certain points of infantry tactics were re-emphasised. The assaulting infantry would advance in waves (to keep close to the barrage) followed by columns; mopping-up and consolidation of captured positions were to be thorough; the tendency to use bombs where rifle fire would do the job better was to be curbed; Lewis guns were to be placed on the flanks and in forward positions; Stokes mortars were to be used as close-support weapons; and both direct and indirect machine-gun fire were to be used from the rear. The last point reflects the development during 1915 of the machine-gun barrage, first used by British troops on the Somme in August, when at High Wood the 100th Machine Gun Company had fired nearly one million rounds from ten guns in 12 hours of non-stop fire. The effect had been devastating, breaking up a number of German counter-attacks before they had been properly launched.

The effect of leaving lanes in the creeping barrage proved fatal to the success of the attack. Heavy enfilade fire from German machine gunners in these areas caused considerable casualties, and not infrequently the infantry were denied even the consolation of the tanks, as they broke down on their way to the front line (only 36 made it there) or were simply late. Much of XIV Corps' assault failed completely, and only on its left was the German front line overrun, after which the attack ran out of steam. XV Corps, in front of Longueval and Delville Wood, made much greater progress, capturing Flers and some positions beyond it; the 12 tanks able to make the attack out of the 17 allotted to the corps had caused panic among the defenders, and later were effective in crushing wire which would otherwise had prevented the move against Flers. The regimental history of the 12th East Surreys described the action:

> Zero hour was 6.20 a.m. Promptly to time our artillery opened a terrific bombardment, and automatically the troops in the front line began to advance behind the creeping barrage, the 12th Battalion followed behind the 18th K.R.R.s [King's Royal Rifle Corps] who could be seen moving to the assault on the first objective, Switch Trench (Green Line), which was taken by 6.30 a.m. The enemy machine-guns began to take toll as the troops advanced across No Man's Land. Reaching the old British front line, the 12th Battalion paused a few minutes and then went on in the direction of Switch Trench. Many casualties occurred at this stage of the proceedings through the men being too anxious to get forward to help the K.R.R.s, whose ranks were becoming sorely depleted through enemy machine-gun fire, which was very severe from the direction of the village of Flers.
>
> The enemy, realising that his front line was gone, now began to bombard it. As the 12th Battalion was coming up to take its positions before the final assault on the village, it suffered rather badly in consequence. Officers and men began to fall right and left.

Reaching the second objective, Flers Trench (Brown Line), the Battalion now linked up with the K.R.R.s after an advance of about 1,000 yards. Very little opposition was experienced in taking the Brown Line, although a machine-gun team in front of A Company caused many casualties before it was rushed with the bayonet. The German survivors in the trench surrendered to C.S.M. Horswell, who had by now taken over some of the remnants of his company, Captain Jessop having been wounded soon after the first objective was reached.

So swift had been the advance that objectives were in advance of the creeping barrage, and very soon the men were caught between the British and German fire. Accordingly Sergt. C.Maguire of the Signal Section set about getting red flares lit and signalling to the planes overhead with panels. The planes, picking up the signals, soon got our artillery to lift on to the village. Some of the enemy retreated in this direction, while others made their way to our lines to surrender.

Meanwhile a tank slowly made its way towards our second objective. Up to now it had taken no really active part in the fighting, unless it was to frighten the enemy. It was a heartening sight to see this machine crossing trenches and deep shellholes as if they had never existed. Nothing stopped its progress, slow as it was compared with the infantry.

Six hundred yards still remained to be covered between the second objective and the village. As the barrage lifted, the 12th Battalion went forward, and, although held up for a little time by some wire in front, managed, with the assistance of one of the tanks, to be the first troops to enter Flers.

Down the battered High Street the men of the 12th made their way, while the tank fired its machine and light guns into German posts which were still holding out in the village... Much confused fighting ensued, as the result of which we lost heavily in officers and N.C.O.s. Some of the Germans threw stick bombs at the tank, but these simply exploded on its sides without doing any damage to the machine or its occupants. The village was actually in our hands before 10.30 a.m. Dugouts and cellars were bombed, and prisoners taken and sent back to the rear. As the trees in the orchards were laden with apples, no time was lost by the men in stripping them...

Those of the enemy who were able to get away made off in the direction of Gueudecourt, and soon after they left the German artillery began to put down a terrific barrage, which caused our troops to evacuate the village. Flers was the third objective (Blue Line) and the final objective (Red Line), consisting of a double line of trenches on the other side of the village, had yet to be taken. With the shelling of the place a certain amount of disorganisation now set in, especially as most of our officers had by now become casualties, but there is evidence that remnants of the Battalion went on, particularly from C Company under Lieut. J.W.Staddon, who was severely wounded in gruelling fighting beyond the village... For the rest it is clear that positions were occupied on either side of the village by different parties from the Battalion. The final part taken by our men after the Germans had made the village untenable is difficult to piece together, as the account in the War Diary is so incomplete as to render it useless as a record of events. This is in the main explained by the fact that the Commanding Officer and all except one of the other officers...became casualties... Consequently we have to turn to the official accounts by the Brigadier and his Brigade Major.

General Towsey [the Br.-Gen. commanding 122nd Brigade] states that, after the village was in our hands, practically all the officers of the Brigade had become casualties, units were all mixed up and there was considerable confusion. There was a tendency to remain in the village instead of pressing on and consolidating. It was noticed that the Germans released pigeons before evacuating Flers and Switch Trench. The village was then heavily pasted with gas shells, and a barrage was placed between Flers and Switch Trench. Touch too had been lost with the Brigade on the right. About 11.00 a.m. groups of men began to go back on our left, and this movement spread along the line. Parties began to drift back towards the Brown Line (Flers Trench), but Lieut.-Col. A.F.Townshend, commanding the 11th Royal West Kents, endeavoured to stop this movement, till he was mortally wounded while consolidating a line south of the village to resist a possible counter-attack...

On hearing that the troops were falling back from Flers and that the situation was obscure, General Towsey sent the Brigade Major at 1.00 p.m. to investigate personally. Major Gwyn Thomas found on arrival that the advance, instead of pushing north of Flers, was stationary south of the village, and it was of importance to get the troops forward. As it was out of the question to advance through the village, which was being intensely bombarded by the enemy, Major Gwyn Thomas ordered Lieut. Carter [228th Field Company RE] to stop his work on the strong points and collect all the available troops of the Brigade west of the strong point and advance on the west side of the village. On the S.W. side of the village the Brigade Major found a tank burning. He then moved west of Flers, taking with him what troops he could collect... Elements of the Brigade followed the Brigade Major to the N.W. of the village and so averted any further withdrawal of troops who had previously advanced beyond the village and were retiring on the left of the Brigade.

The reinforcements advanced successfully to a point roughly 300 yards to the north-west and 100-150 yards north of the village, where flares were lit at 2.00 p.m. Here enemy rifle fire was encountered. Some New Zealanders with a machine-gun north of the village were also ordered to move forward and consolidate on the line about 100-150 yards nearer the enemy.

North-east of the village was a derelict tank, and here a party under Lieut. Carter and a Vickers gun under 2nd Lieut. Gilliat were directed by the Brigade Major to take up a position to cover the village close to the cross-roads, where there was considerable sniping. Passing back east of the village, Major Gwyn Thomas returned to Flers Trench and ordered forward further reinforcements, including a company of the 124th Brigade, to north of Flers. These dispositions rendered the village comparatively safe from counter-attack, as, in addition to the infantry with Lewis-guns, 5 Vickers guns had been pushed forward by the Brigade Machine-gun Officer. At about 4.15 p.m. the 123rd Infantry Brigade took over the line, and what was left of the 122nd Brigade was gradually withdrawn...

In the area around Flers, the whole of the German second line had been captured. III Corps, however, suffered grievously as its commander, Lt.-Gen. Pulteney, decided that the tanks would capture High Wood and so expanded the area not covered by the barrage to include that feature. How the tanks were expected to negotiate the tree stumps is a mystery. Only when the wood had been outflanked and heavily shelled by mortars could it be cleared. Francis Buckley, of 7th Northumberland Fusiliers, recollected that:

Unfortunately High Wood was not taken by the 47th Division on our right till midday, and meanwhile we lost heavy casualties from having our right flank exposed to machine-gun fire.

Finally, the Canadian Corps had succeeded in capturing Courcelette. Overall, the German front line had been captured on a front of 9,000 yards, and the second on one of 4,000; Courcelette, Martinpuich, High Wood and Flers had been taken. But casualties had been heavy - about 30,000 - and no breakthrough had been achieved. The French had fared still worse, achieving no significant advance at all.

Minor operations followed, with an attempt on the German third line planned by 4th Army for 21st September, though it was postponed until 25th owing to bad weather. Reserve Army was to take the ridge running from Courcelette to Thiepval, in an attack planned for the following day. The 4th Army operation, preceded by a bombardment almost twice as dense as that on the 15th, and against weaker defences, was an almost complete success. Morval and Lesboeufs were taken on the first day, and Gueudecourt and Combles on the second. However, lack of reserves and of French success prevented a further advance, despite the current weakness of the Germans. To the left, Reserve

Army's operations led, by 30th September, to the capture of most of the Thiepval Ridge, and the Thiepval Redoubt, which had been an objective on 1st July. It was finally captured by 18th Division, under Major-Gen. Ivor Maxse, which had also been one of the most successful divisions on the first day of the offensive.

Needless to say, while the fighting in September had been raging, the Germans had been busily constructing further defensive lines behind those being captured by Reserve Army, 4th Army and the French. These were the objectives in the subsequent fighting on the Somme. Little was gained, as the weather deteriorated and mud hampered the troops. An artillery officer wrote home:

> On the 18th, we attacked again at 3.45a.m. and fired without a pause all day. The same evening it started to rain, and for thirty-six hours without a break the skies did their worst...

> Maclean and I sleep in the mess, and we woke up to find a vast pool at the ends of our bed bags; also, as usual, the trench outside had had a landslide, which on this occasion thoroughly blocked the exit from the mess. After breakfast we waded about in mud over our knees, trying to repair things. The back of No.1 gun-pit had fallen in, half-burying the gun, and No.2 pit seemed to have bred a spring during the night and was nearly a foot deep in water. We spent the morning rescuing ammunition from the worst of the water and patching up the dug-outs and gun-pits... As it did not clear up in the afternoon, we did a little blind shooting at registered targets, and then I walked over into Delville valley to see Major Stanley, and found him in an even worse plight than we, as besides the mud, they had been heavily shelled all day...

> The rations came up [that evening] in a S.A.A. limber, and although it was a light load for four horses, they managed to get finally stuck four hundred yards from the guns. Musson took some men down and unloaded it, but as bad luck would have it, soon after a close shell made the horses plunge, and the horses and empty limber capsized into a vast crater which was filled with liquid mud. After three hours' work they rescued the horses, but the vehicle had disappeared into the muddy depths of the crater. To make matters worse, while on their way back carrying the contents of the cart, one of the men got stuck in the road, sinking up to the waist in a shell hole, and it needed a passing ammunition mule and a drag rope to 'yank' him out. Incidents like this are of daily or rather nightly occurrence.

> As the night was pitch dark and a big relief was taking place on our front, we had more than our usual share of inquiries from lost souls wandering helplessly about the country. That night I left before dawn, meaning to reach our forward saps by 7a.m... The going was really bad,

and one was literally waist deep in mud in the trenches for the last 600 yards, and we found two infantrymen completely overcome with exhaustion and stuck in the mud half-drowned. You can therefore understand how it sometimes takes two or three hours to do a journey of 3,000 yards. [Lt. Col. N.Fraser-Tytler]

In addition to the mud, British difficulties were increased by a further change in German tactics. Their machine-gunners were pulled back to positions beyond the usual range of the creeping barrage, but still close enough to reach the attacking troops. This caused heavy losses in the unsuccessful attacks of early to mid-October, even though the problem had been identified and gunners advised to extend the creeping barrage for the whole depth of the German position. One theory as to why gunners were slow to react to this advice is that the conditions made ammunition supply difficult and so they simply lacked the shells to move the barrage further. Their problems were not simply confined to the mud, however:

With our worn guns and three different sorts of powder, all of which is more or less damp, it is impossible to expect accurate shooting by paper calculation, however carefully one may work out atmospheric and all other corrections. Consequently we are now great believers in jamming our noses as close as possible to the target, loosing off a salvo, and then to business. [Lt. Col. N.Fraser-Tytler]

The problems of the infantry were greater still:

That afternoon preparations were complete. Three companies, about 270 strong in all, were to do the frontal attack. Seven officers remained for these three companies. They were to start from a taped line that I had had put out the night before, parallel to Rifle Trench, about 300 yards from it, in front of New Cut. They were to go in two lines, with men about 2 yards apart, and only a few yards between the lines. One Vickers gun, from my old company, went with them, and they took their Lewis guns. They were to try and join up with the bombing attack up Snap Trench, on the left...

There was to be no preliminary bombardment, but the guns were to open on Rifle Trench at 2.45, and lift after 3 minutes, when it was hoped we should be across... Steady rain had settled in for some hours, and the trenches were in a bad state. The were dug in clay, and were slimy and water-logged. I went along to the right of the line, to check the tape and the company fronts. The piece of Bind Support between Snap Trench and New Cut had been shelled out of recognition many times: and bits of it were mere tracks over mounds of clay. It was mostly too narrow for two men with equipment on to pass.

I scrambled and slid along this, and was soon covered in clay wash and slime. I tried to be cheery with the men as I passed; but it was perfectly obvious they were out of heart, after their long exposure to shelling and with the atrocious weather conditions. Their rifles were nearly all unworkable with clay, and they knew it; and that took the heart out of them too...

I got back to the dug-out, and first took off the jersey I was wearing, as the sleeves had come down over my wrists and were simply solid with clay...

The minutes went by. Then at last there was a crash and a roar, and the bombardment had broken out. Soon I went up to see what I could see. I walked a little way along the trench and looked over the parapet towards Rifle Trench... It was hell out there - shrapnel bursting, bombs exploding, our own barrage further on - it was one long crash and roar. And the Verey lights were going up in large numbers from Rifle Trench; and then I clearly saw, silhouetted against the Verey lights, some little black figures running - back. The attack had failed...

It was some time before I got any direct news from the right. What had happened, however, was that the lines had gone across - somewhat raggedly perhaps, owing to the ground and the conditions - that they, or a great part of them, arrived within 30 yards of the Boche trench and collected in shell-holes, finding the trench full of Germans, who were keeping up a barrage of bombs; that out of 7 officers who started with the three companies 5 were by that time hit; that while the left began to waver under machine-gun fire and rifle fire, the right was thinking of charging in - when the left broke and went back and the rest followed. There were between 100 and 150 casualties among the men.

I think the attack was too light to have much chance against a full trench. The other elements of failure were the weather conditions and the worn-out state of the men. [Major H.F. Bidder]

Under these conditions, further attacks were bound to be costly and unlikely to succeed. One more large-scale operation was launched by 5th Army (as Reserve Army was retitled on 30th October), on both sides of the River Ancre, in which Beaumont Hamel fell. But a shortage of manpower compelled offensive operations to be suspended. The campaign was officially closed on 19th November. Much had been learned in the four and a half months of fighting, for every division in the BEF bar two had fought on the Somme, sometimes on several occasions. While Rawlinson and Haig seemed at times not to be able to absorb the lessons of the last attack, their subordinates could. But the cost was about 420,000 casualties to the British (and the Empire troops) and 200,000 to the French. German casualties are harder to establish, but estimates range from 400,000 to 680,000.

5
Development of the Set-Piece: Arras and Messines

At the end of 1916, which had opened so full of hope engendered by the advent of the New Armies, stalemate still prevailed on the Western Front. The army high command claimed that the Somme had been a great victory, for (they asserted) the cream of the German army had been destroyed and only the knockout blow was needed to finish off the reeling German forces. But the politicians were unconvinced, feeling that even if the German army had been devastated, the price in British casualties was unacceptably high. The rift between the 'frocks' (as generals tended to refer to politicians) and the 'brasshats' was exacerbated by strategic disagreements. The writers of memoirs after the war (especially Lloyd George) portrayed this split as one between 'easterners' and 'westerners'. Most of the high command were said to be convinced 'westerners', believing that the only place where Germany could be defeated was the Western Front. On the other hand, the 'easterners', including the Prime Minister, Lloyd George and Winston Churchill were alleged to feel that an indirect approach, of destroying Germany's allies in other theatres such as the Middle East and Italy and so 'knocking away the props' supporting the German war effort would be far less costly in time and lives. This was not the case. The dispute was really between those who felt that Britain should stick to her traditional policy of a limited commitment to the land war in Europe, and support her allies through financial, industrial and naval means, and those arguing for the most vigorous possible use of all the country's resources, irrespective of social or financial cost, in order to secure total victory in as short a time as possible. The latter group, who by 1916 had won the debate, included both the generals and radicals like Lloyd George and Churchill. Nevertheless, after the Somme, there was a growing distrust of the generals in some political circles. The gulf between the two groups was exacerbated by personal dislike, Sir Douglas Haig distrusting politicians in general, and Lloyd George in particular as underhand schemers, and the latter viewing Haig and his fellows as stupid, callous butchers. And so 1917 began with a far from satisfactory relationship between the army and its political masters, which the events of that year did nothing to improve.

As a result of their lack of progress in 1916, the French government were also disillusioned with their generals. Joffre was dismissed, and replaced by General Robert Nivelle, who had enjoyed success in his limited operations in 1916. His plan to end the war in 1917 essentially involved breaking through the German lines at Arras and in the Champagne region in order to nip off the huge salient protruding into France by penetrating it at the base of each flank. Nivelle was a charming and plausible man, and received the backing not only of his own but also the British government. To Haig's consternation, he was subordinated to Nivelle by the despised 'frocks' and instead of launching a great offensive in Flanders early in the year, he was required to assist in the Nivelle plan by attacking around Arras, further south.

However, the Nivelle offensive was doomed from the start. Concerned by their losses in 1916 at Verdun and on the Somme, the Germans decided to shorten their line by 25 miles and so free more troops for the reserve; 14 divisions were in this way released. In mid-March 1917, they withdrew to the carefully prepared and immensely strong 'Hindenburg Line,' as the Allies referred to it. As they went, they devastated the countryside and took with them anything and anyone of value. The only civilians left behind were the old, the very young and the sick. The British were slow to realise that the withdrawal would happen, and the pursuit was not as vigorous as it might have been; but the skills of open warfare were not great in armies which had spent two and a half years ensconced in trenches. Lt.Col. Fraser-Tytler took part in the pursuit:

> From the 12th [March] to the 15th we saw an unusual number of the enemy walking outside their communication trenches, and on the 16th... I heard that not a single hostile gun had fired all day, and that very few Huns had been seen. Also, after dusk, the glare of many fires could be seen in the east. While playing Poker that night, the news came in that the enemy had evacuated Monchy, a front line village about five miles to the south. I felt convinced that he had gone from our front, and just before dawn went down to our front line, having first extended my wire from the O.P. further back. A sergeant told me that his Company had gone across No Man's land some time before, so, leaving a signaller with the telephone at our front line, I started off, meaning to establish visual signalling across the 500 yards which separated us from the old German strong point called "The Block-house".

I got through our barbed wire without difficulty, in fact in that section it would not keep a healthy chicken in, but while crossing No Man's Land the company on the right opened a brisk but inaccurate rifle fire on me. They were evidently in blissful ignorance of the morning's happenings. Being unarmed I was unable to reply to their fire, but fortunately the light was very dim, and we were not seriously inconvenienced.

I reached "The Block-house" at last and found that our people had only just occupied it. They were a new Third Line Division just out, and seemed to be chiefly employed in collecting souvenirs in the intervals of taking cover from the intermittent fire from our lines. A message was signalled back visually to request the company to stop firing at us, and then some young officers turned up and asked me to point out their positions on the map, as even in that short distance they seemed to have lost their bearings. As they all had revolvers at full cock there was a short interval for necessary precautions before I felt inclined to start my map-reading class.

At this stage of the proceedings two resolute Hun bombers could easily have cleared us all out, as dispositions for the defence of the new front appeared to be nil. Their major, however, turned up at 6 o'clock and got a move on things generally, and a little later the Brigadier, a real good sort, appeared, and detailed the barrage lines he wanted in case of attack, as the enemy were still to be seen on the ridge behind.

On being relived by a subaltern at .8 o'clock I returned to Brigade Head-Quarters for breakfast. Orders and counter-orders all day. Some of the other B.C.'s [Battery Commanders] and my F.O.O. explored far into Hunland, often a thousand yards in front of the infantry, and yet no signs of the Hun could be seen. Our teams came up that night at 9p.m., and we dumped the guns down in a position about a thousand yards behind the old British line. I spent the night in a comfortable cottage belonging to Major Sarson's Howitzer battery, which had not moved.

Next morning, the 19th, Major Sarson, myself, and my reconnoitring officer, Wilshin, went mounted to try and get in touch with the enemy, and to find out if it was possible to get the guns along to a certain valley. The roads and bridges across the trenches were being repaired with great energy, but in every road, and especially at cross-roads, there were 20-foot deep mine-craters, so it was not easy to scheme out a way to advance. The Hun had, besides, left every sort of booby trap. There were helmets with bombs underneath them, bunches of bombs behind half-closed dug-out doors, detonators under dug-out steps, enticing iron boxes which exploded when the lid was opened, and many roads ready to blow up as soon as traversed by a vehicle. The R.E., however, did wonderful work in spotting quickly and removing all these toys, and I did not hear of a single casualty.

We had a topping gallop across clean grass country till we reached a point 4½ miles from our old front line, and then rifle and machine-gun fire from the village in front warned us that it was time we ceased to be cavalry. Leaving our horses to be watered and fed in a deep donga, we walked to the village of St. Boiry Marc. The main street was rather unhealthy with enfilade machine-gun fire, so we worked our way through the ruined houses till we reached our advanced posts, which were facing the enemy in Boiry Becquerelle...

The hinterland is certainly a wonderful sight. Only the grass is left, that had proved too much for the Hun to destroy or to remove, but every village is razed to the ground, every tree cut down and the roads blown up. I noticed a few willow trees still standing, but nearly all the hedges are levelled, and the rails and sleepers are gone from the railway tracks.

Although this withdrawal effectively removed the salient in the German line which Nivelle's plan had been intended to nip out, he nevertheless insisted that the attacks go ahead.

*   *   *

The British component of Nivelle's plan, the Arras offensive, was conducted by 1st and 3rd Armies (under Horne and Allenby, respectively). From the French point of view, the broad intention of the attack was to draw in the bulk of the German reserves before the main French assault on the Aisne - although given the size of the British forces involved, this hope seems rather forlorn. The British 1st Army was to capture Vimy Ridge, near Lens and just south of the BEF's battles in 1915. The main attack would be delivered by 3rd Army, on a front extending from just south of Vimy Ridge to Beaurains, south of Arras. The total length of both armies' front was about 12 miles. The first day's objectives went as far east as the village of Monchy-le-Preux; on the second, the Drocourt-Quéant switch, a defence system created as a northern extension of the Hindenburg Line, was to be taken. After this ten-mile advance, the new German defences could be outflanked and exploitation follow. As so often in the previous year, Haig differed with his army commander as to the length of the preliminary bombardment. Allenby, who had, in the many tunnels and underground chambers in the area a means of concealing large numbers of men, wished to retain the element of surprise by having only a two day bombardment (in fact, this would still have alerted the Germans). He was overruled, his MGRA replaced, and a five day bombardment was used, preceded by a week of 'unobtrusive' (it was

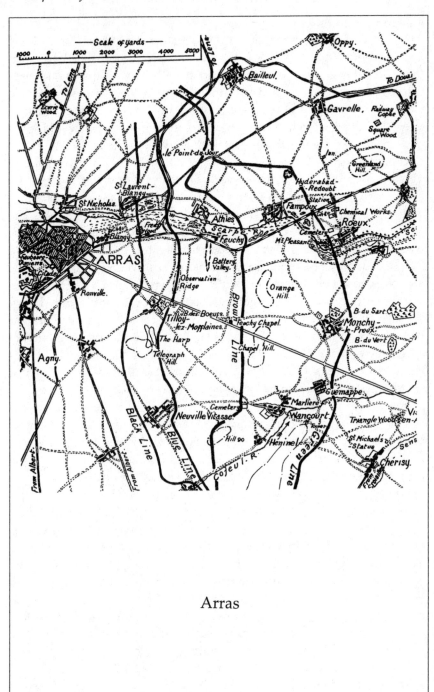

Arras

hoped) wire-cutting fire.

The attack was to be made by the Canadian Corps on Vimy Ridge, and from north to south, XVII, VI and VII Corps. After they had taken their first day's objectives, XVIII and the Cavalry Corps would pass through the centre and drive on to the switch line. One new feature was that XVII and VI Corps were to attack on a front of three divisions; after the third objective was taken, a fourth division would pass through to take the fourth and last of the day's objectives.

Unlike some of the Somme attacks, artillery was not in short supply. The total of guns and howitzers available to 3rd Army was 1,720, and a higher proportion than in 1916 could be used for the barrage, since Stokes mortars were to be used to cut wire within their range. The tendency just to attempt to saturate the enemy positions with shellfire was replaced by a system where each battery fired on defensive localities in assigned map squares, making observation easier since the area to be watched was more specific. Each type of gun was given tasks commensurate with its range and calibre. For example, the heavy artillery in particular was concentrated on counter-battery work (at times using the newly available gas shells), while the creeping barrage was to be fired by 18-pounders, moving forward at a rate of 100 yards every four minutes. Another innovation was that at zero hour a standing barrage was to be fired by 4.5" and 6" inch howitzers on the support line of the enemy front line. When the creeping barrage reached this point, the standing barrage would move on to the next objective. Between these two, 60-pounders would fire on places where German riflemen or machine-gunners might be concealed. One problem, however, was that aerial observation was difficult in April 1917; the Germans enjoyed a technical edge which gave them air superiority, and the month became known to the RFC as 'Bloody April.'

However, the artillery was not completely blinded, since two other techniques for locating German batteries were available. These were 'sound-ranging' and 'flash-spotting'. The first had been developed by an artillery subaltern, Laurence Bragg (who was already a Nobel Prize Winner) between late 1915 and late 1916, and depended upon the positioning of a row of microphones in the required area. These picked up the sound of a German gun's report and the flight of the shell. When fully developed, the system could identify not only the position of the gun, but also its calibre and muzzle velocity. Flash spotting enjoyed a shorter life, since the Germans began to use flashless propellants during 1917, but it nevertheless was a useful innovation. A team of observers, arranged in a row, would all signal electronically when they saw the flash of a gun, whose position could then be calculated using trigonometry.

The by now obligatory machine-gun barrage was also to be fired over the heads of the infantry, and as they advanced, machine-gunners would follow in order to set up a new barrage on the next objective. This was by now the main role of the Vickers gun; the Lewis was usually employed for close support of the attackers, though some Vickers were also brought forward to deal especially with counter-attacks.

The final element in the attack was the tanks. Forty were used, though they were not involved in the attack on the first objective, since that was not viewed as difficult. As on the Somme, they were to assist in subduing strongpoints and operated in small groups.

The assault began at 5.30a.m. on 9th April. Despite terrible weather - snow flurries and a bitingly cold wind - the attack went well. In less than an hour the whole German front line was captured, and the Canadians took Vimy Ridge, despite its formidable reputation, derived from the numerous unsuccessful French assaults upon it earlier in the war. While not belittling the Canadian achievement, it is only fair to point out that the Germans had not yet put into place a deep defensive system on the ridge, and so the front trenches held a high concentration of defenders, ready to be swept away by the creeping barrage. North of the River Scarpe the success continued, and the 'leapfrogging' of divisions proved effective as 4th Division of XVII Corps went forward to secure the village of Fampoux. Within that division was the 1st Rifle Brigade, which captured a position southeast of that village, known as the 'Hyderabad Redoubt.' The regimental history gives the following account, largely from the diary of an officer in the battalion:

> The 11th Brigade was formed up with two battalions in front - 1st Bn. Somerset Light Infantry and 1st Bn. Hampshire Regt. - and the 1st Bn. East Lancashire Regt. in support. "The role of the Battalion [1st R.B.] was to pass through this system and capture and consolidate Hyderabad Redoubt. 'A' and 'C' Companies were to do this, supported by 'B' company, whose job it was to occupy the sunken road between the Fourth German system (i.e. the Fampoux-Bailleul road) and the redoubt and make a line of strong points along it. 'I' Company was detailed for carrying purposes only and was under the Brigade.
>
> On the evening of the 8th we were in camp at Marœuil Wood. Here

there was an observation balloon up and when it came down we asked the observer if he could see the results of the bombardment. He said that although he had been observing there for over two years he could not recognize the first two German lines; that the fourth line was badly knocked about and he could not pick out the Hyderabad Redoubt at all...

We started off at about 5.30 a.m. (Zero hour) on the 9th, heavily laden with picks, shovels, bombs, etc., Schiff's orderly carrying a football tied to his rifle. The Battalion went into action with Head Quarters and three companies totalling thirteen officers and three hundred and forty-two other ranks...

After a two hours' wait at our assembly area... we left at 10.30 and in column of route, crossing the original No-man's land and halted for an hour behind the second German system under the Arras-Lens railway embankment (The Blue Line). By this time we knew that things were going well; masses of prisoners had passed us going to the rear and our artillery was moving forward to take up [new] positions.

Our next move was in artillery formation on a two-company front until we reached the third German system, where we had to halt for over two hours, to allow for a new bombardment... The 34th and 9th Divisions told us they had practically no fighting for this third system..."

Towards the end of this halt, at 3.10 p.m., the Somerset Light Infantry and Hampshires assaulted and captured the enemy fourth system whilst the East Lancashires formed a defensive flank facing north...

"Our show... started at 3.40 p.m. and we moved in artillery formation of platoons on a one company front following behind the Somerset Light Infantry. After about one thousand yards we extended to battle formation. When we came over the ridge in front of the fourth system we came into the German barrage, and as it was extremely thin we had hardly any casualties at all [the use of the new gas shell in counter-battery work had proved to be most effective, especially since its lethal effect on the German gunners' horses meant that they could not bring up more ammunition]. We had great difficulty in getting through the German wire, which was forty yards thick in places, as our artillery had completely failed to cut it. The Boche was so anxious to give himself up and we were so anxious to get in that the confusion which reigned was so bad that no one could move either way through the gaps that did exist.

It will always remain a mystery why the Boche put up no fight here. The wire was unbroken in front of them and a couple of machine-guns could have held up the advance of the whole Division. One hundred and forty prisoners were taken in the fourth system."

Soon after getting through the fourth system "we came under machine-gun fire from an inn on the Rœux-Gavrelle road and from Gavrelle. We soon managed to pick out the redoubt on account of the masses of wire which surrounded it, which we could see was completely intact... When we came within twenty yards of it the football was drop-kicked by Corporal Bancroft into the redoubt and the place was rushed. The various mopping-up parties under Bridgeman started clearing the dug-outs and after a time seven officers and nine men appeared. A staff officer tried to bolt down the road to Gavrelle and was at once shot by 'C' Company's sniping corporal."

Meanwhile "B" Company had been dropped at the sunken road where it quickly mopped up the dug-outs and itself occupied trenches just east of the road which, incidentally, proved to be the enemy barrage line.

"The consolidating parties got into position quickly and outposts and patrols were sent out. These, however, and all parties outside the redoubt were heavily fired upon by the Germans who were lying out in the open between the redoubt and the Rœux-Gavrelle road and had organized their snipers very quickly."

In the brigade report on the operations, doubt is expressed whether troops so recently in a state of complete demoralization could have been re-organized so quickly; the view is put forward that these were fresh troops brought up from the rear who had rallied the retreating survivors of the garrison.

"The patrols could make no headway and the consolidating parties were being picked off one by one, so everyone was withdrawn inside the redoubt and all efforts were concentrated on consolidating the place... Up till dark we got several good targets for rifles and Lewis guns and there is no doubt that the enemy suffered heavy casualties. These undoubtedly would have been considerably heavier had not the ammunition almost entirely run out..."

By this time it was getting dark. Germans were closing in on the north, south and east faces and had begun digging in a semi-circle 200-400 yards off... A counter-attack by two battalions was seen coming from the direction of Gavrelle. This attack was not pressed home and came under heavy fire from our artillery...

The redoubt was occupied at about 4.30 p.m. and by 3 a.m. on April 10th the situation was fairly secure and touch had been gained with the 12th Brigade on the right. During the 9th a total of ten officers - including a general and his staff - and thirteen other ranks had been captured, also three heavy howitzers, a travelling kitchen, a machine-gun and much telephone equipment and a mass of official documents, orders and maps. Our casualties that day were Jackson and

Schiff killed; Cavendish, Bridgeman, Day and Wellard wounded... and one hundred and twenty-three other ranks killed, wounded and missing...

The Battalion reached and held the furthest point of the whole British advance. It was a great day full of excitement and interest and was chiefly remarkable for the utter demoralization of the Boches and more especially for the extraordinary way in which the advances were made exactly to time, according to the time-table laid down; it seemed far more like one of the many rehearsals than one of the greatest battles of the War."

No defences now lay between the attackers and the Drocourt-Quéant switch in this sector. However, south of the Scarpe, VI Corps was badly delayed by stiff resistance, especially round Monchy-le-Preux. It was in this area that the cavalry were expected to move forward, and so they vainly waited as instructed, adding to the considerable congestion in and around Arras. The plan was insufficiently flexible and communications too difficult for them to be moved to the north instead; the successful units there were not reinforced on the first day. Nevertheless the 3rd Army had advanced three to four miles, the largest distance in one day since the onset of trench warfare.

The next day, the offensive was renewed, but not until 11th April did Monchy-le-Preux fall, and by then the Germans were rapidly moving up reserves. Once again, the attack stalled, and further attempts to break through foundered. The lessons were twofold; firstly, that poor communications denied senior commanders flexibility, and secondly, that although the artillery could help the infantry win in a limited, set-piece attack, once advances of any magnitude were undertaken, it was a terribly slow process to bring the guns forward and get them ranged on new targets, and hence the momentum of the attack was all too easily lost. Nevertheless, the experience gained on the Somme had led to a considerable initial success.

The main fighting in the Arras sector ended on 15th April. However, the French attack on the 16th was so unsuccessful compared to Nivelle's predictions of a great and decisive breakthrough, and casualties so high that a large portion of the army mutinied, and they were effectively out of the war for several months. In consequence, small scale attacks by the British continued on the Arras front until June, with 5th Army supporting 3rd. It was clear that maintaining pressure on the Germans from now on was to be the job of the British, with relatively little French support. In fairness to the latter, it should be noted that they had taken on the main burden of fighting until the Battle of the Somme. Between August 1914 and June 1916 they had suffered two and a half million casualties, whereas the BEF had taken 600,000 over the same period - less than one-quarter of the French figure.

*   *   *

Haig had nurtured the idea of an offensive in Flanders since early 1916. In addition to the possibility of expanding the Ypres Salient in order that the Germans could not then shell it from all sides, or even breaking through to the Channel coast, there was also the consideration that the northern part of the line was perilously close to the BEF's lines of communication to the Channel ports and from them to England. Hence, pushing the Germans back in Flanders would make the BEF's position far less vulnerable. And if the Channel coast were cleared, the Germans would be deprived of their submarine bases in Belgium, the vessels from which were inflicting terrible losses on British shipping (the fact that they would still have had bases in the Baltic seems to have been ignored). The first stage of any such offensive had to be the seizure of the ridges around Ypres. Only then could the attackers move out to cut rail communications with the coast, force the Germans to evacuate much of Belgium, and attempt to roll up their defensive line from north to south.

As a preliminary to the main 'push,' the battle of Messines was intended to improve the attackers' position by seizing the Messines Ridge, in the south of the Salient. Then the main attack on the Gheluvelt plateau would have its southern flank secure. This was accomplished by Sir Herbert Plumer's 2nd Army on 7th June, the culmination of tremendous efforts in planning, organisation and training, all of which characterised Plumer's meticulously thorough approach to operations.

The key to the operation lay in the exploding of 19 (21 had been prepared, but two failed to explode) mines underneath the German lines, containing a total of one million pounds of high explosive. Their preparation had taken years and at times involved vicious hand-to-hand fighting in the tunnels under the trenches and No-Man's-Land. Once they had been detonated at 3.10a.m. on 7th June, II Anzac (in the north), IX (in the centre) and X Corps (in the south) would advance to take their objectives. As at Arras, each corps attacked on a frontage of three divisions, with one in reserve. The whole ridge was to be captured, from Mount Sorrel in the north to St. Yves in the south, but this was an operation with strictly limited objectives; no breakthrough was intended. On a ten mile front, the depth of advance was to be no more than one to two miles.

Once again, tanks were to be employed to help in the capture of strongpoints. However, the 72 allotted were the new Mark IVs, which, while still exhausting and dangerous to operate, were a definite improvement on the Mark Is used previously. The armour and transmission had been improved, as had observation, and an 'unditching beam' was fitted. The latter was a large piece of timber which could be fastened across the tank's tracks if it lost traction. Some Mark Is were also used, to carry petrol, water and ammunition forward.

The main bombardment was fired from 21st May onwards. While the artillery plan was largely based on experience gained on the Somme, the first day's success at Arras had not gone unheeded, and as in that battle, the gunners fired according to a strict timetable on specific targets, and counter-battery work was stressed. No less than 2,266 guns and howitzers were to be used; 756 were heavy and more than a quarter of these were assigned to counter-battery fire. In order to trick the Germans into disclosing the positions of any concealed artillery they might have, two practice barrages were fired in the days preceding the attack. Considerable air support was used in order to spot these hidden batteries.

The changes in German defensive tactics which had evolved under the stimulus of the fighting on the Somme had now been formalized. Three defensive zones, rather than lines, were established, each being two to three thousand yards deep. In the forward zone, instead of holding their front line strongly, they held outpost positions with machine-guns and relatively few men, backed up by belts of barbed wire and concrete pillboxes carefully positioned for mutual support. The bulk of a forward division was positioned largely at the rear of the forward zone and in the second zone. They were protected from artillery fire in protective shelters, and were ready to repel an attacker before he could consolidate his position. Should the second zone be penetrated, specific counter-attack divisions, which were kept out of artillery range (in the rearward zone), were provided in the ratio of one to every two forward divisions. Consequently, in addition to

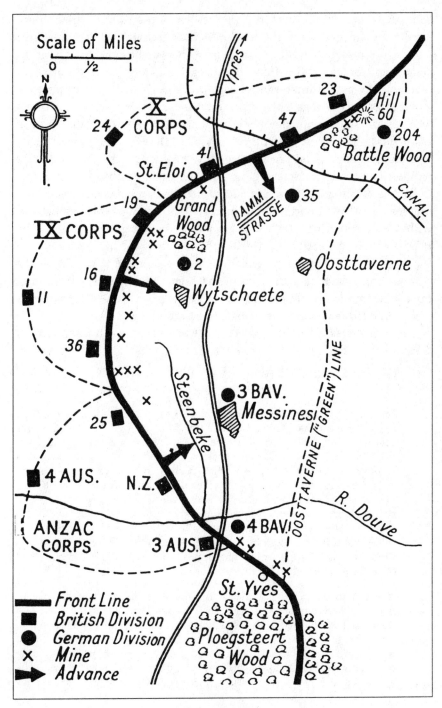

Messines

counter-battery fire, the British artillery used the preliminary bombardment to destroy the machine-gun posts and strongpoints and harass the forward divisions by shelling their communication trenches and other routes to the front line, depriving them of supplies and relieving troops. Counter-attacks were to be dealt with by the creeping and protective barrages accompanying the attacking troops. Mortars were used to deal with the small outposts in the forward zone and to assist the field artillery in wire-cutting. The effect of these preparations was enhanced by good weather and the position of the forward zone on the slope of the ridge facing the attackers, making observation easy.

For the attack itself, creeping and protective barrages were to be fired much as at Arras. In addition, a machine-gun barrage was again used, with 700 guns firing 400 yards ahead of the creeping barrage. The infantry more generally used a technique employed at Arras only on Vimy Ridge (for dealing with deep dug-outs). On encountering strongpoints which had survived the barrage, their loopholes were fired upon with mortars, rifle grenades and Lewis guns, while other groups of infantry moved round the flanks and stormed them.

The attack was a complete success. At the appointed time the mines were detonated (the shock was felt in London) and the barrage began. Anthony Eden recounted in his memoirs his battalion's part in the battle:

> By 2 a.m. we were in position, tight-packed in our limited space, then the Germans began to shell, not heavily, but enough to make me fear that they had spotted us. The repeat of a barrage such as they had put down a few hours earlier on our now crowded ranks would have been murderous. The battalion was tight-packed in this way as deliberate policy, because we wanted to get all companies forward so as to be clear of our front line within seconds of our zero hour, before the enemy's barrage came down upon it, as it had and would. We lay dead still for our lives, the shelling fell away and all was quiet until, just before our mines were due to explode, a spread of rockets and Very lights were fired from the German front line opposite to us; too late, for almost at once the men who had fired them were dead.

> At 3.10 a.m. our mine exploded under the old mine craters and we leapt from our first line under cover of the barrage. The colonel and I were on the battalion's left flank with our headquarters, as near our mine as we dared be. It was an astonishing sight, rising like some giant mushroom to a considerable height in the air before it broke suddenly into fragments of earth, stones and timber falling over a wide area. The whole ground heaved so violently that for a fraction of a second we

1. Early trench near Ypres, 5th November 1914. Note its shallowness and the cabbages to its front; the Salient had not yet been completely ravaged by shellfire.

2. Bombing party, 20th May 1915. The troops appear to be preparing 'jam tin' bombs. Steel helmets had not yet been adopted.

3. Early gas protection, May 1915. In this picture of a gas drill, note the use of goggles and the bottles of Hypo (for dampening the pads). The man just right of centre is wearing a facemask respirator and incorrectly operating a Vermorel Sprayer in an attempt to render the notionally approaching gas ineffective.

4. 8" Howitzers on display, 1916.

5. 8" Howitzers in action, 29th August 1918. These are a later model than in the previous picture. Note the dust rising from the ground as a result of the concussion of their firing.

6. First day of the Battle of Amiens, 8th August 1918. A single Australian leads a large group of German prisoners past the burning remains of their dugouts.

7. German machine-gun team in open country. These troops were the mainstay of the German defensive effort by late 1918.

8. 9.2" Howitzer in place under camouflage netting before the Battle of Arras, 1st April 1917. The shells do not yet have their fuses screwed in.

9. Messines Ridge under bombardment, June 1917.

10. 'Caterpillar' towing 60-Pounder gun covered in camouflage netting.

11. 60-Pounder gun firing at dawn. Battle of the Canal du Nord, 27th September 1918; note the field artillery going forward, silhouetted at the right of the picture.

12. Wrecked German 8.3" howitzer in Bourlon Wood.

13. A formidable obstacle; German wire in front of the Hindenburg Line, near Arras.

14. Stokes mortar position in early 1918. The waterlogged conditions show the need for the waders worn by the man in the foreground.

15. Battle of the Lys; an impromptu Lewis gun post near Merris, 12th April 1918. The gun's magazine is being changed.

thought we were over the mine instead of beside it. As the barrage opened simultaneously, the noise of the guns deadened all sound from the mine, except that we could hear, even above this crescendo, the screams of the imprisoned Germans in the crater.

We could do nothing for them, for we had at all costs to keep up with our barrage. Our tactics were based on a close follow-up by the infantry to allow enemy machine-guns no pause to get into action before we were upon them. As it was, we captured a crew with what appeared to be a new type of machine-gun intact in one of the craters. Presumably they were too shaken by the mine explosion to do their job in time, but we had no illusion about the casualties that gun must have inflicted if it had got going. When the riflemen cleared the dug-outs which had not been blown in, they found watches hanging on nails which they avoided as possible booby traps, and hot tea and 'reindeer' sandwiches which they ate.

We found few enemy survivors among their forward positions, but it was at this early stage that I came upon the only fatal casualty I witnessed among our riflemen that day...

For the rest of that day our attack succeeded beyond our wildest dreams. The Dammstrasse [trench] on our front had been virtually obliterated, as Harington [Plumer's chief of staff] had promised, and the Fusilier battalion on our left captured their stretch without loss. Even so, the dug-outs built into the bank and invisible from our side were immensely strong. Evidently we owed much to those 9.2s [i.e. 9.2" howitzers]. As my official War Diary succinctly recorded in its final sentence on the day's fighting: 'The artillery bombardment and the barrage were excellent.'

So was the staff work. During the five hours which our advance was planned to last, we were scheduled to attack a series of lines, red, blue and black on our maps. The rate of our advance and the length of the pause at each captured objective was perfectly timed to give us just long enough to regroup before the barrage moved on again and the enemy no sufficient opportunity to rally and fight back.

Those five hours were, after the first roar, scramble and confusion, a carefully ordered and executed advance, exactly as we had so repeatedly rehearsed. In the brilliant June sunshine I felt a rising sense of enthusiastic astonishment, of incredulity almost. This was so utterly unlike anything we had experienced before and so different from what we had expected. Despite all the practice attempts to convince us, we had not really believed at any time that we could capture all our objectives. If I had been asked before the battle what my inmost thoughts were, I should probably have said that we would be doing well if we captured the foremost organized trench system...

It was still only just after eight in the morning when we reached our final objective and saw dramatically spread before us on the ground the consequences of capturing the Messines ridge. On our immediate front the enemy was retiring his guns and infantry. This was a target such as we had never had in our sights before. Two companies of riflemen opened concentrated fire and the casualties the enemy suffered in the next half-hour were probably the heaviest of the day in this sector. I watched as the withdrawal became hurried and disordered under that raking rifle and Lewis-gun fire.

Our orders were to dig in when we had captured our final objective and prepare to meet a counter-attack. In the early evening we were to be relieved by a battalion of the Buffs from another division. No counter-attack developed. On the contrary we urged that our victorious gunners should be brought up to deal with the target now retreating beyond our range.

With the cynicism of a young man who though himself old in battle, I remarked to the colonel that for sure we could not be relieved in such an advanced position that day; we would be lucky if our relief came at dawn. Once more I was proved wrong. The Buffs arrived on time to an eager welcome.

As we marched back in evening light over the ground we had captured and were nearing our old front line we saw our happiest sight of the war; our gunners had limbered up and were galloping forward over the old trenches on a hastily prepared way, up and on and over to take up their new positions and fire again upon the enemy we had just left. How we waved and shouted and cheered, for this had been their day.

When we got into camp that night, tired out as we were, we just had to discuss the events of the day. There were tales of a resounding victory and of thousands of prisoners. Our excitement was intense and we began to think that we were winning the war, that it might even soon be over. A pardonable illusion surely, but it was not to last long. Next morning I was able to make our own contribution to the general good news. Our casualties had been very slight; a total of seven killed and sixty-four wounded which included the ten casualties, three killed, of the night before the attack. We had no certain tally of the prisoners captured, but a first batch of eighty had been taken in the early fighting up to the Dammstrasse and about fifty more in the advance to our final objective.

Eden's battalion was in X Corps; his experience was repeated all along the line. Even Messines village, a notable stronghold, was overrun with the aid of tanks. Casualties only began to mount because far fewer than expected had been suffered at the start of the attack, and with the arrival of more troops the ridge became congested with men and so more targets were presented for those German guns surviving the attentions of the British artillery. However, German counter-attacks were beaten off with artillery and machine-gun fire and the day ended with the most complete victory for either of the Allies since the trench lines had been established. Fighting continued until 14th June, when the Germans evacuated the few positions remaining to them at the base of the ridge. The Battle of Messines demonstrated how careful planning and preparation, and the application of sophisticated infantry and artillery tactics could make a set-piece attack succeed completely.

6
Good Tactics, Bad Ground: Third Ypres

After Messines came the Third Battle of Ypres (often referred to as Passchendaele), infamous for its weather, terrain and loss of life. It is probably the most controversial battle of the war, generating acrimony even within the team of official historians writing about it in the 1930s and '40s, to the extent that one of them refused to put his name to the relevant volume of the Official History. Even today, no definitive account of the battle has been written.

From the start it was an ill-starred operation. Plumer had been pressed by Haig to follow up the Messines attack immediately with another, just to the north, with the intention of establishing a foothold on the Gheluvelt Plateau. However, the 2nd Army commander asked for a three-day postponement in order to move artillery up from Messines. At this point (8th June) Haig decided to hand the new attack over to Hubert Gough, who was viewed as a 'thruster' with the verve and offensive spirit associated with the cavalry (in which he had begun his career). In addition, it had already been decided that 5th Army would conduct the main offensive in the area, for which the attack under discussion was a preliminary stage. Despite having had plans for this operation passed to him by Plumer, Gough decided that it should be included in the main offensive, and received Haig's backing. As a result, the opportunity rapidly to follow up the success of 7th June, and catch the Germans when they were relatively weak, was lost, as were precious time and good weather.

The offensive had originally been conceived as depending on French support to draw German reserves away, but after the mutinies this was no longer forthcoming; indeed, the strategic idea changed to the attitude that it was necessary to keep German pressure off the French. The politicians were very wary of sanctioning another Somme, preferring to divert resources to Italy and the Middle East, while waiting for the Americans (who had declared war on Germany on 6th April) to arrive on the Western Front. However, Haig and Robertson assured them that only limited attacks with a good chance of success would be undertaken; this gained the War Cabinet's grudging acceptance, despite the possibility of Russia (in the throes of the March Revolution) dropping out of the war, so freeing additional German troops to fight in the west.

In fact, Haig viewed the new offensive as an attempted breakthrough, although Rawlinson, Plumer, Gough (but see below) and even Haig's own chief of operations (Br.-Gen. John Davidson), favoured a series of methodical, set-piece attacks with limited objectives. Given the comparative inactivity of the Russians and French, they were reluctant to incur casualties like those of 1916, lest the BEF run out of men before the Americans arrived in strength. Nevertheless, as ever, Haig's idea was the one adopted; in fairness, during the planning of the battle he had Gough's backing too, the latter viewing a breakthrough as feasible if made in the first 48 hours of the attack. After a great deal of discussion - not to say wrangling - between Gough, Haig, Neill Malcolm (Gough's chief of staff), Plumer and Davidson, a plan was arrived at which was acceptable to the C-in-C. Gough proposed to advance north-east on a broad front, from Steenstraat in the north to Observatory Ridge in the south, and penetrate the German defences to a depth of two miles in the initial assault. If this went well, subordinate commanders were ordered to advance further to Passchendaele, although under what precise circumstances was left unclear. However, and despite reminders from GHQ on this point, the frontage of attack was to narrow as the intermediate objectives were gained. Consequently, much of the commanding feature of the Gheluvelt Plateau, from which counter-attacks on 5th Army's right flank could be launched, was not to be taken, and the attacking troops would be more vulnerable to hostile shellfire than on a wider front.

In fact, only the forward zone of the German position could be directly seen, and 5th Army's gunners were heavily dependent on aerial observation. The very nature of the Salient meant that the Germans, holding the high ground around its rim, had direct observation for their heavy and medium artillery, and could conceal it behind those ridges. The attack at Messines had enjoyed the advantage that the ridge had formed a salient protruding into the British lines, and could thus be shelled from three sides; now the Germans had this advantage, and on a larger scale. Consequently, counter-battery work before the attack was difficult, and further hampered by the Germans moving their batteries frequently. Aerial observers were deceived into thinking that successful shelling of the gun-pits they could see meant that German artillery was being destroyed, when they were in fact empty targets. In addition, the Germans' excellent observation over the Salient made their counter-battery fire more effective. While 5th Army was using 3,091 artillery pieces, it was opposed by over 1,500 which were in a position to hamper preparations for the attack considerably. These problems were exacerbated by the effects of the ten day long preliminary bombardment on the drainage system of an already boggy area, which reduced much of the ground to be attacked to the consistency of a thick sludge, which would exhaust men moving through it to attack, and make bringing supplies forward a major operation. The intensity of the bombardment was the greatest thus far in the war, and over 4,250,000 shells were fired on a 15-mile front. No tactical innovations for artillery, infantry or tanks were employed; this was to be the biggest set-piece attack to date, notwithstanding its planners' hopes of a breakthrough.

While 2nd Army made feint attacks on its right, 5th Army advanced at sunrise (3.50a.m.) on 31st July, on a four corps front (XIV, XVIII, XIX and II, from north to south). The first three of these were to form what the Official History calls a 'northern defensive flank'; the main attack, by II Corps, was to establish a foothold on the Gheluvelt plateau. However, by the end of the day, the attackers were less than half-way to their objectives, and had lost 30 to 60% of their fighting troops. Initially the advance had not been difficult; the war diary of 16th Rifle Brigade described the fighting in the XVIII Corps attack:

> The Battalion advanced at zero hour in artillery formation - the front platoons being fifty yards behind the rear wave of the preceding battalion... The enemy barrage came down on our assembly position at zero plus eight minutes, but by this time the Battalion was crossing the German front-line trench and so escaped it. Direction was well maintained and the Battalion formed up behind the barrage at the Dotted-Blue Line waiting to advance. Up to this time the Battalion had suffered few casualties.

> At zero plus 1 hour 23 minutes the Battalion advanced to capture the Black Line. The formation now was the first two waves in extended order and the last two waves in artillery formation (by platoons).

> Racecourse Farm offered serious opposition to my left companies... as it had a machine-gun in a concrete emplacement which offered resistance and inflicted serious casualties till the last. This position was rushed and the machine-gun captured and eight enemy killed. A mopping-up

company left behind captured another two Germans. My left company was fired at by a machine-gun from Bochcastel Estaminet. This was silenced by rifle-grenades and Lewis-guns.

The leading wave advanced into Cannon and Canoe Trenches (Black Line) and was fired on by several machine-guns and snipers in Kitchener's Wood. One machine-gun was giving a great deal of trouble and... was captured with two prisoners: rifle-grenades and Lewis-guns were used in the capture. Two officers of my Battalion... were killed by this machine-gun.

My right company was fired at (during the advance to the Black Line) by a machine-gun which was in a concrete strong point built in the open (in the re-entrant outside Kitchener's Wood). This was dealt with and the gun captured with eight prisoners and two wounded prisoners. This concrete emplacement was splendidly camouflaged and was not shown on any map. The size of the emplacement was about 6 feet high and had an area of 20 feet by 30: the concrete was from 18 to 24 inches in thickness and withstood our barrage...

Kitchener's Wood was cleared and my leading companies advanced to, and dug in on, the Black Dotted-Line. Snipers and machine-guns were encountered in this wood and the enemy there either killed or captured. During consolidation machine-guns were active from Regina Cross, Alberta, and another emplacement.

The two rear waves now passed through the Black Dotted-Line and advanced to the protective barrage ready to attack the Steenbeek. These two companies were now in extended order and advanced with the barrage at zero plus 3 hours 40 minutes (7.30 a.m.).

Regina Cross, which consisted of three strong points, offered serious resistance to my left company by heavy machine-gun fire. Platoon tactics were used in enveloping it by pushing round the flanks and using Lewis-guns, rifle-grenades, and No. 27 phosphorous grenades. These positions were then rushed from all sides and the garrison of about thirty was killed, or captured. Three machine-guns were taken also. Little further opposition was met with until the Steenbeek was reached and crossed at 8.01 a.m., when a machine-gun opened fire from the extreme left flank. This position was rushed and the machine-gun and four prisoners captured.

After capturing the Steenbeek a line was consolidated about thirty yards beyond, and Lewis-guns pushed out in front to cover the consolidation. This line was dug and the men under cover by 9.00 a.m. At 8.07 a.m. a contact aeroplane came over which called for flares; these were lit by the most advanced troops.

This account shows well how infantry tactics had improved in 1917; the

Official History states that Stokes mortars were also used in the capture of Regina Cross. However, it also brings out the difficulty for observers in aeroplanes or officers studying aerial photographs in spotting every pillbox. A feature of Third Ypres was the discovery by attacking troops of well camouflaged positions, the existence of which had not been known before.

Although the attack of 31st July initially went well, and the forward zone had been captured to a depth of one mile, it bogged down under heavy German artillery fire and counter-attacks. On this and the next two days, casualties totalled 31,850. Worse still, heavy rain had set in by the end of the first day; this was to continue, with some breaks, until the end of August. The battlefield became a quagmire, and the Steenbeek, running across its centre, a swamp. Artillery observation was also hampered since low cloud made it often impossible for aeroplanes' observers to see the ground. The flares referred to in the preceding anecdote may well not have been seen, since the relevant corps (XVIII) report on the day's fighting states that from 4.13a.m. onwards 'no further reports were received throughout the day from aeroplanes owing to adverse weather conditions.'

Not surprisingly, 5th Army's attacks during August made comparatively little headway; at times, the infantry were so hampered by mud, that they were left behind by the creeping barrage. As on 31st July, tanks were employed, but were completely unsuitable for the ground. Major Watson of 'D' Battalion, Tank Corps (the latter was officially formed on 27th July 1917), described the fate of an attack on 28th August:

> It was lonely on the Poelcapelle Road, with nothing for company but shells bursting near the tanks. After the heavy rain the tanks slipped about on the broken setts, and every shell-hole in the road was a danger - one lurch, and the tank would slide off into the marsh.
>
> Very slowly the tanks picked their way. Three tanks reached the cross-roads. The fourth, Lloyd's, scraped a tree trunk, and the mischief was done. The tank sidled gently off the road and stuck, a target for the machine-gunners. Two of the crew crept out, and the unditching beam was fixed on to the tracks. The tank heaved, moved a few inches, and sank more deeply. Another effort was made, but the tank was irretrievably ditched, half a mile from the German lines.
>
> Three tanks turned to the right at the first cross-roads, and, passing through our infantry, enfiladed the shell-holes occupied by the enemy. The effect of the tanks' fire could not be more than local, since on either

side of the road were banks about four to five feet in height. The enemy were soon compelled to run back from the shell-holes near the road, and many dropped into the mud; but machine-gun fire from the shell-holes, which the guns of the tanks could not reach effectively, prevented a further advance.

One tank moved south down the track towards the strong points, but found it blocked by a derelict tank which the enemy had blown neatly into two halves. My tank remained there for an hour, shooting at every German who appeared. Then the tank commander tried to reverse in order to take another road, but the tank, in reversing, slid on to a log and slipped into a shell-hole, unable to move. One man was mortally wounded by a splinter.

The barrage had passed on and the infantry were left floundering in the mud. The enemy seized the moment to make a counter-attack, two bunches of Germans working their way forward from shell-hole to shell-hole on either side of the tank. Our infantry, already weakened, began to withdraw to their old positions.

The tank commander learned by a runner, who on his adventurous little journey shot two Germans with his revolver, that the second tank was also ditched a few hundred yards away on another road. This tank, too, had cleared the shell-holes round it, and, bolting the garrison of a small strong point near it with its 6-pdr. gun, caught them as they fled with machine-gun fire.

There was nothing more to be done. The tanks were in full view of the German observers, and the enemy gunners were now trying for direct hits. The tanks must be hit, sooner or later. The infantry were withdrawing. The two wretched subalterns in that ghastly waste of shell-holes determined to get their men away before their tanks were hit or completely surrounded. They destroyed what was of value in their tanks, and carrying their Lewis guns and some ammunition, they dragged themselves wearily back to the main road.

The remaining tank, unable to move forward as all the roads were now blocked, cruised round the triangle of roads to the north of the strong points. Then a large shell burst just in front of the tank and temporarily blinded the driver. The tank slipped off the road into the mud, jamming the track against the trunk of a tree. All the efforts of the crew to get her out were in vain...

Meanwhile, we had been sitting drearily near Divisional Headquarters on the canal bank, in the hope that by a miracle our tanks might succeed and return. The morning wore on, and there was little news. The Germans shelled us viciously. It was not until my tank commanders returned to report that we knew the attack had failed.

When the line had advanced a little, Cooper and I went forward to reconnoitre the road to Poelcapelle and to see our derelict. Two of the tanks had been hit. A third was sinking into the mud. In the last was a heap of evil-smelling corpses. Either men who had been gassed had crawled into the tank to die, or more likely, men who had taken shelter had been gassed where they sat. The shell-holes nearby contained half-decomposed bodies that had slipped into the stagnant water. The air was full of putrescence and the strong odour of foul mud. There was no one in sight except the dead.

The offensive had stalled by the end of August. While the preceding narrative makes it clear that this was partly the result of a number of factors out of their control, the poor performance of 5th Army's staff and Hubert Gough himself also contributed - even simple matters such as the burying of telephone lines so that they would not be cut by shellfire were neglected. The focus of the attack was moved south, into the hands of Plumer, who had, after all, been based in the Salient since late 1914 and knew the ground well; 5th Army was to make advances corresponding to those of 2nd, but in a supporting role only.

Characteristically, Plumer proposed to capture the Gheluvelt Plateau in a cautious series of step-by-step advances. Four were to be made, each with definite and limited objectives and extending to a depth of about 1,500 yards. This was to allow as much field artillery as possible to be brought forward for the next stage, about six days later. The medium and heavy artillery was ordered to pay particular attention to the destruction of concrete shelters and pillboxes, and to counter-battery fire. There was a three-week pause in the fighting (and the rain) while the first phase was prepared, and the next major assault, on the Menin Road Ridge, took place on 20th September. Captain H. Raymond Smith of 11th Battalion, Rifle Brigade, took part:

> My company was in support, so we did not go over with the first wave at dawn the following morning, but held ourselves in readiness, and it was one of the most trying days I have ever spent. We were obliged to stand or sit in a large "pill box" or in a narrow slit trench immediately at the rear of it. At 6 p.m. I got the order to advance. What followed will forever be imprinted on my mind as the most vivid recollection of all my experiences in the Great War.
>
> The sun is shining brightly, and the enemy trenches are about seven hundred yards ahead. I hastily issue a rum ration to my men, and we leap out of the trench and start forward at the double. M— and I lead the way, the company following us, almost in single file. No sooner do we emerge from the trench than all hell breaks over us! The bursting

shrapnel crashes above our heads, and great shells plough up the ground all round, sending up huge fountains of earth and flames. The ear-splitting scream is continuous, and the bursting shells shake the ground. I glance round and wave the men forward. They are struggling gamely along, carrying their rifles and Lewis guns, slipping into shell holes, falling and rising again. Bang! Something like a blow from a hammer strikes my steel helmet, and I double forward all the faster. We are under machine gun and rifle fire now. An orderly rushes up to me and thrusts some papers into my hand and I start to read them, with the bullets whistling all round, my heart pounding, and expecting every minute to be my last. Before I have had time to take in the sense of a single word, the orderly snatches the paper from me and shouts "'A' Company are going over, sir, and I've got to stop them." With this he dashes across the road. The men of "A" Company, on my right, leap from a shallow jumping-off trench, but they do not get far. In a moment they are falling - being doubled up like shot rabbits, before a deadly hail of machine gun bullets. This fire is now taking its toll of us. M—, who was close by me a moment ago, has gone, and several others. I dash across the road and take shelter in the trench just vacated by the ill-fated "A" Company. With me are Sergeant T— and two riflemen; the remainder are sheltering behind a "pill box" to our left rear. I send Sergeant T— back to tell them to join us as soon as possible, and turn my attention to our immediate position. "Your sergeant's been hit sir," says a man from another unit. I turn and see Sergeant T— on the ground, some thirty yards away. I jump out of the trench and go to him. One glance shows the damage. A bullet has torn his right wrist open and another has gone through his left shoulder, and already his tunic is soaking in blood. "Leave me, sir; I'm dying," he says, to which I reply "Don't be a fool." Kneeling beside him I get his equipment off, and with his right arm over my shoulder I get him to walk with me towards the trench again. All the time bullets are zipping round, and the centre of a cone of fire from a machine gun ploughs up the earth in a shower just on our left, but we reach the trench in safety. S— and T—, the two riflemen who have remained close to me throughout the advance, bandage the wounded sergeant up with their field dressings, and I give him two morphia tablets, and write "2M" on his forehead in accordance with instructions.

At last it is dusk, and we are joined by the rest of the company, now sadly depleted in numbers. M— has been killed, and W—, my second in command, has gone, wounded, I am told, and I am the only officer left. Presently the Commanding Officer and Adjutant arrive, and I am instructed to occupy the left flank of Eagle Trench. We move forward under the cover of darkness, and do so. This Eagle Trench is curiously situated, as it is now partly occupied by us and partly by the enemy.

Our position is by no means comfortable. The enemy are in strong force just on our right in a "pill box," which is a strong point in the trench, and I am determined that so far as I am concerned they can stay there, for the time being at any rate, as by this time I have only about forty-five men left at my disposal. The first thing I do is to build a barricade in the trench between us and our enemy, and having posted a sentry here I inspect the rest of our position, which, to put it mildly, is far from healthy.

That night was cold, but dawn came at last, and with it a renewal of the shelling. Our own gunners must have thought the whole of this trench was occupied by the enemy, for they started shelling us, and it was most disconcerting to be under fire from both front and rear. The dauntless S— and his pal at once volunteered to go back to Battalion Headquarters, and I gave them permission to do so. To accomplish this perilous journey they had to crawl or sprint from shell hole to shell hole, as the ground was constantly swept by machine gun fire. We had only our emergency rations with us, but we were able to get a little extra food and water during the night, by taking the water bottles and iron rations from the many bodies lying around. My two volunteer messengers returned late in the afternoon and dropped into the trench rather breathless, but smiling. Wonderful fellows! They told me that we should be relieved tomorrow, and this was good news for all. My message had evidently been passed back to the batteries, for our shells no longer dropped short.

We were relieved by a company from the 10th [Rifle Brigade] early on the following morning, and retired under cover of darkness to the support line. Under pressure from three sides the Germans in the "pill box" surrendered; there were over eighty of them. T—, who was acting as my batman, presented me with a handsome pair of field glasses, which he had taken from one of the prisoners. He said he had "won" it. Our Battalion was relieved early on the following morning. D—, who was in command of "A" Company, and I left last, under cover of a thick white September mist. On all sides, as we made our way back, were dead bodies and heaps of rifles and equipment.

Despite Raymond Smith's misgivings, the attack was a success. Changes in infantry tactics went some way to countering the German defences. Now concealed strongpoints which had escaped the preliminary bombardment and the creeping barrage were unmasked by a line of skirmishers (who were also to deal with German troops sheltering in shell-holes) and then assaulted by the rifle grenadiers and Lewis gunners as before. In the meantime, other such groups worked between strongpoints to deal with the next line of defences. When the existence of a strongpoint was known before the attack, a specific section or sections was assigned to deal with it. This represented a large transfer of responsibility to junior officers and away from battalion commanders or higher. When a position had been gained, the attackers would obviously have suffered casualties and be tired; hence the function of Raymond Smith's men - to move up behind the main attack in order to deal with the inevitable counter-attacks. A further innovation was that, in order to avoid the overcrowding which had occurred at Messines by the sending forward of unnecessary reserves, their deployment was to be left to the commanders on the spot, rather than (for example) divisional commanders further back, whose knowledge of the situation would necessarily be imperfect.

The artillery power behind these new tactics was massive; for the 20th September attack, the density of fire was four times that on 31st July. In and before its assault, XVIII Corps (actually in 5th Army) fired no less than five different types of barrage, and varied the speed of the latter according to the degree of opposition (and hence delay) likely to be encountered. Firstly, the 18-pounder field guns fired the creeping and protective barrage which as well as shrapnel and high explosive, employed smoke shell in order to conceal the attackers; this also had the benefit of making the defenders suspect that gas was mixed with the smoke and so they encumbered themselves by putting on gas masks. Then other 18-pounders and 4.5" howitzers fired the combing barrage, which was to dwell on strongpoints and work up communication trenches. Six-inch howitzers and 60-pounder guns fired the neutralising barrage, to search beyond the combing barrage. Fourthly, the standing barrage was fired by heavy howitzers and 60-pounders, in order to reach even further into the defences and break up formations of troops preparing to counter-attack. Lastly, during the 24-hour preliminary bombardment as well as in the attack, a 'draw net' barrage was fired. This consisted solely of high explosive shells and started 1,500 yards behind the German front line, moving slowly back to the latter, where it paused for ten minutes. Then shrapnel was fired, as if an attack was about to start. Since it was used twice before the assault was actually made, it was most confusing (as well as lethal) for the defenders. And all this was backed up by mortar and machine-gun barrages.

Under such circumstances, it is not surprising that the attack was a success, although casualties were heavy. Almost all objectives were taken, and counter-attacks either prevented by artillery fire or beaten off. German artillery fire was made less effective by counter-battery fire, often including gas shell, and by the infantry taking a leaf out of the Germans' book and not consolidating on trench lines, but holding an outpost line on the final objective and having their main position among the strongpoints of the second. And the responsiveness of the artillery was enhanced by bringing wireless sets to some of the OPs and to all brigade HQs. Lastly, although it rained on the 19th, the weather was dry and sunny on 20th September, and had been for most of the previous three weeks.

The battle continued, with losses mounting as further successful set-piece attacks were made on 26th September and 4th October, and more of the Gheluvelt Plateau was captured. On the latter date, the old front line of winter 1914-5 was reached. And on the same day, the weather broke again; the last phase of the battle was the one which contributed most to its reputation as a struggle against the mud as much as the Germans. Conditions grew steadily worse; Lt. Col. Fraser-Tytler wrote of the difficulties of moving forward in late October:

> Next morning, the owners of the guns we were looking after reappeared, so that we were able to concentrate all our men on pulling our own out of their pits and getting them to some spot where they would not sink out of sight while waiting for their limbers; we also tried our hardest to make some sort of a track by which we could reach the main road.

> By noon the staff, having at last realized that the R.E. could not possibly make the road along the Broombeck within the allotted time, directed that B Battery and ourselves were to go and hunt for a place forward from where we could fire during the battle. Emsley, O.C. of B Battery, and I therefore plunged off through the mud once again, and eventually discovered a small piece of ground about 50 yards long, just off the road at Widjendrift. There we could just wedge in the two batteries, but it was in full sight of the Hun, and with the muzzles poking through a long screen erected to hide the traffic on the road behind us - an absurd place, but in this paradox of war it had to do. It meant however, handing over to C Battery all the ammunition we had packed up to the Broombeck with so much labour, and criminally hard work it had been, too, on the wagon line, as each trip meant fourteen hours at least on the road, and often longer, with but few hours' rest between trips.

> I wonder if guns have ever been moved before across such impossible country? C Battery, which had its old position 200 yards behind us, started to advance early in the afternoon, but by dark had only managed to move five guns as far as our position, when every horse and man were absolutely beat. Rather slow progress in the march to Berlin!

> Here is a typical example :- Six 8-horse gun teams had left the wagon line at 10 a.m.; they reached the block on the road behind our position by 4 p.m., and getting the vehicles reversed and trekking back, only as

far as our advanced wagon line, took them till 10 p.m. They started off at 3 a.m. next morning, and the crater having been filled up they reached us at 9 a.m.; from then till noon was one long fiendish struggle to move the guns across the 300 yards to where the timber road began. It was desperate work - one gun at a time - fresh teams into each gun every 50 yards, and every man on the drag-ropes - the whole job being done under fairly heavy shell-fire. Once on the timber road, however, it was good going as far as Widjendrift, but then another desperate struggle began to get the guns hauled on to their new platforms, which were erections of scrap timber built between shell-holes, on which the guns perched like rickety sparrows. It was the best we could do, as the background all round was pulp... At 5.35 a.m. on the 22nd [October], the attack on Houthulst Forest began. It was a horrible morning of driving rain and mist, and it was a perfect miracle that our infantry ever advanced at all, but somehow they managed to, and captured the fringe of the forest, thus robbing the Hun of observation of our immediate area. Our task in the barrage was a simple one, assisting in the forming of a second creeping barrage in front of the main barrage. Luckily for once extreme accuracy of fire was not essential, as we had not been able to register the guns, which slid about everywhere on their impromptu platforms, and now and then kicked themselves off their perches, sinking immediately axle deep in the mud.

With the reduced accuracy of the artillery, and the difficulty of getting ammunition forward through the mud, barrages were much less effective, and so were the attacks. Although the offensive continued into November (finally being halted on the 12th), hopes of a breakthrough had long since been abandoned. Initially this had been in favour of a battle of attrition, to weaken the Germans to the extent that one last blow would be all that was required to finish them off. Later, it was continued in order to win Passchendaele village and ridge as a jumping-off point for operations in 1918 and a comparatively dry place for the troops to winter in, without being under direct German observation. In the event, the village was captured on 6th November, but the position gained was in a narrow, indefensible salient.

British and Colonial forces had suffered much for a relatively small improvement in their position and an advance of no more than five miles. Even the aim of taking the pressure off the French was of dubious value, for their army had largely recovered from the mutinies by July, and even took part in the battle, on the British left flank. The BEF's casualties amounted to about 250,000; the Official History asserts that the Germans suffered about 400,000, though its pronouncements on German casualties should be treated with caution. At least, however, it was now evident that the BEF's artillery enjoyed considerable technical superiority over the Germans' (in contrast to 1914), and that with the improvements in infantry tactics, any defensive position could be broken into. The problem now lay in breaking through.

It was not Haig's fault that the offensive had been delayed as a result of his being compelled to fight at Arras, as part of the Nivelle plan. But the Ypres area was simply not the right place to attack when the opportunity for action independently of the French (for the first time in the war) arose. And the problems inherent in the terrain were exacerbated by confusion regarding the aims of the offensive. Haig fell into still deeper disfavour with the government and he was forced to despatch troops to Italy, struggling to stay in the war after successful Austro-German attacks. Nevertheless, he was permitted one more offensive on the Western Front in 1917 - the Battle of Cambrai.

7
Shooting off the Map: Cambrai

Ideas for a surprise tank attack were first proposed early in 1917, and during August and September there was much discussion between GHQ, the Tank Corps staff and 1st and 3rd Armies as to where and when the attack should take place. Eventually a plan for a limited raid using a large number of tanks was accepted and Sir Julian Byng of 3rd Army convinced GHQ to let it take place in his part of the line. For the task he was given seven infantry divisions (with two more in reserve), five cavalry divisions and three tank brigades. The Hindenburg Line was to be breached on a six-mile front between the Canal du Nord on the left and the Canal de L'Escaut on the right. The infantry (IV and III Corps) and tanks would capture the ridges of Flesquières and Bourlon, which dominated the area, while the Cavalry Corps moved on to Cambrai, seven miles behind the front. This break in the Hindenburg Line would expose the Germans to the risk of having their line rolled up to the north, and, if deep enough, such a breakthrough could threaten the whole German defensive system. Furthermore, Cambrai was an important rail junction, and its capture would cause the Germans considerable problems. It seems that the idea of a simple raid was quickly forgotten.

The plan had a number of novel features. The first, and most important, was that the attack was to be a surprise. Elaborate precautions were taken to conceal the men and material involved, and no preliminary bombardment was undertaken. Instead, 'shooting off the map', or 'predicted' fire was used. In previous attacks, the gunners had registered the artillery on their targets beforehand, by firing ranging shots at them, since they lacked the accuracy to set their range, direction and trajectory by assessing the target's position on the map relative to theirs and making allowances for the idiosyncrasies of the gun or howitzer and its ammunition and for the effect of other factors, such as wind speed and direction. By November 1917, it had been realised that each artillery piece varied slightly, and so they were calibrated against a standard before issue. By the same token, batches of ammunition also had variations, and these too could be allowed for. This meant that no ranging shots were required and so the number and positions of the guns could be hidden from the enemy far more easily. And improvements in mapping meant that the relative positions of gun and target on the map were now accurate.

The second new feature was that the bombardment would be relatively brief and only commence when the attack itself did. Instead of destroying the enemy defences over a week or more, and in the process cratering the ground to such an extent that it was difficult for the attackers to advance, it was simply intended to cut the wire and keep the Germans in their dugouts until the infantry got to them in order to mop up survivors. A new fuse, which had seen service at Third Ypres, was to be used extensively. This 'fuse 106' was sensitive enough to detonate the shell on impact with the wire or the ground, rather than after it had dug in, so cratering could be avoided and the blast went outwards rather than upwards, making it more effective than shrapnel for wire-cutting.

The third novelty was that tanks were to be used in large numbers for the first time. A total of 476 (of which about 100 were support tanks) were put into the attack, most of which were Mark IVs. They were to crush the enemy wire, making lanes for the infantry to pass through (further eliminating the need for a lengthy preliminary bombardment) and assist them in destroying strongpoints and machine-gun posts. Rfmn. Aubrey Smith, a driver in the London Rifle Brigade, was stationed in the Cambrai sector before and during the attack:

> The first indication we had that our quiet sector was to be the scene of unusual happenings was the arrival of a staff officer who wanted an estimate of the maximum number of men each building in our camp would hold at a pinch. To our surprise and amidst general subdued protest, he put down about fifty for the Nissen huts, fourteen for the sergeant's tent, forty for the harness room and twenty for the wash-house. It was confidentially whispered that there was to be a secret concentration of troops on this front, and that, as the erection of fresh camps would arouse suspicions on Bourlon Hill [i.e. amongst German observers there], the existing buildings had got to harbour everybody...
>
> Day after day went by without hearing further news of the coming battle, but one night we noticed some guns coming up the Cambrai road to take up positions which our astute camouflage brigade evidently

considered well-concealed, in spite of Bourlon observers and German aeroplanes. In order to disarm suspicion it was impossible to concentrate more than a few extra guns or to allow them to register on targets before the battle began, since surprise seemed the essence of our operations.

Presently the battalion, who were in camp at Lebucquiere, were told that the surprise attack would shortly take place without any artillery preparation, the way being prepared for the infantry and cavalry by masses of tanks. The most ambitious objectives were attributed to the scheme. They spoke of advancing six miles the first day, making the gap we had so often heard about, passing cavalry through to surround all the garrisons of the Hindenburg Line and then marching on, unobstructed, into the heart of Belgium. Of course, the announcement and rumours were received with derision and many sarcastic comments. We had learnt in a very bitter school the folly of expecting too much and under-estimating our opponents' strength.

On the other hand, the more we heard about the scheme the more plausible did it sound, in spite of our conviction that nothing much could be done before the winter. It was the news about the tanks which cheered us. These engines of war, which had been improved within the last twelve months, had never been given a real chance, as the mud up at Ypres had been so serious as to restrict them to the roads. Here there was hard, dry ground and their chief role was to plough lanes through the vast fields of wire that protected the Hindenburg Line, destroy the machine-gun posts and clear a way for the infantry and cavalry, the latter having a splendid terrain before them, practically free of shell-holes. It certainly seemed feasible, but we must have a good number of divisions that could be poured through the gap.

The first day (20th November 1917) of the attack was an unprecedented success. The German position was breached to a depth of three to four miles, over 4,000 prisoners were taken and 100 guns captured or destroyed. British casualties amounted to no more than 4,000. One divisional observation officer wrote:

> At 8 a.m. we sent down a report to brigade and to divisional headquarters that we could see that the first Hindenburg system was completely captured all along our front, that the tanks and troops were advancing towards their second line of trenches, and that everything appeared to be going well.

> About this time the enemy appeared to be completely demoralised; prisoners were pouring in. An officer prisoner stated that they had expected an attack near Havrincourt. They had learned about this from the statements of our prisoners taken in a raid. He also told me that the Germans were preparing to make an attack on this sector themselves, and that the billets in the local villages had all been allotted to their

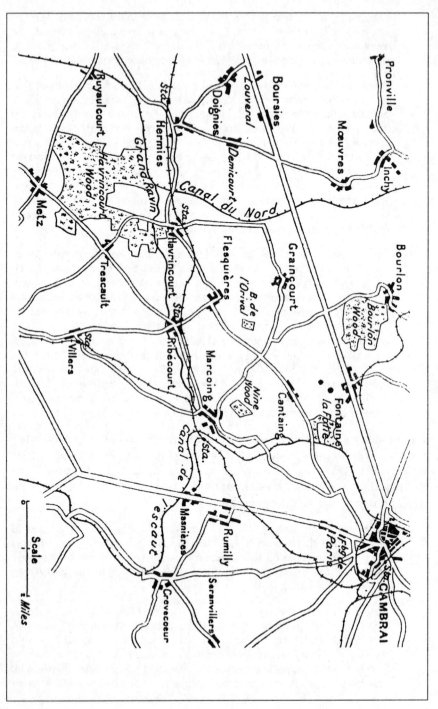

Cambrai

storm troops.

About 9-40 a.m. all the German shelling appeared to have ceased. We viewed the battle from the top of our observation post; behind us great activity prevailed; for the first time we saw the magnificent spectacle of our field artillery limbering up and going forward, first at the trot, then at the gallop, battery after battery, to take up new positions on the captured German front line.

This was the first time that we had ever seen the artillery moving forward. It gave us all a great thrill; this attack of ours seemed to be developing into a great victory. At the same time the 29th division behind us received orders to go through to attack our last objectives. A far as we could see on the right they marched, three brigades in line, each battalion in fours. I cannot describe in words what a wonderful sight it was. The only thing missing was a band in front of each battalion. We cheered.

Battery after battery of artillery moved off at a gallop to take up new positions. The special tanks for clearing the wire trundled up and down the Hindenburg Line catching up the wire with hooks and rolling it into huge balls, so that it should not get in the way of our cavalry, who were to come up shortly.

At 10-40 a.m. we could see our tanks and troops entering the village of Marcoing; also we could see in front of us the tanks advancing towards the top of the Flesquières Ridge; we could see that the village of Flesquières had not yet fallen. This was most important news, so a message was sent to division and headquarters to acquaint the Generals of this fact. It meant that we were right through the Hindenburg Line, and advancing into the open country beyond.

General Duncan told me afterwards that this message was so incredible, that so far as he was concerned he sent it forward adding a note to say he could hardly believe it. I think the powers that be waited for this information to be confirmed before they ordered the cavalry forward. In fact, it was not until 12-30 p.m. that the cavalry received orders to advance.

All this time we could see our troops digging in to make their positions secure. The Flesquières Ridge in front of us was a wonderful sight, shells bursting in all directions. Many tanks at this time were on fire on the ridge, the German batteries firing at them almost at point blank range. Near the village of Villers Plouich we could see masses of men working hard constructing a light railway and repairing the roads for our transport and heavy guns to come up.

About this time the first of the cavalry started to arrive, and a wonderful sight they were. Regiment after regiment passed us going down the valley on our right. When they got behind the lines occupied by our troops they dismounted, waiting for orders under cover. By their arrival it looked as if we were going to make a push right through to the rear of the German lines; but more of this later.

Motor machine gun corps and cyclists were also pushing forward, and at about 1 o'clock squadrons of the cavalry passed through the front of the 29th division to capture the two villages of Cantaing and Noyelles, which lay more than four miles behind the original German line.

By this time civilians from the villages of Marcoing and Masnires were coming back through our lines, carrying what possessions they could save on their backs, driving cows and pigs in front of them. This was the first time that any of us had taken part in such a victory. We felt exalted. [Captain Geoffrey Dugdale]

While the defences of the Hindenburg Line were massive, the British, with over 1,000 artillery pieces of all types, were undoubtedly helped by the opposing German *54th Division* only possessing 54 field guns and no heavies. The tanks got over the trenches, which were both wider and deeper than normal, by carrying 'fascines' - enormous bundles of wood, held together by chains - which they dropped into them and used as bridges. However, problems soon arose. The village of Flesquières was not taken on the first day, owing to poor infantry-tank co-operation (for which Byng must be held partly responsible, since he did not take steps to ensure a uniform approach to this). And the cavalry was mishandled and came up too late to take full advantage of the Germans' confusion. The whole operation had been conceived as limited in scope, to be broken off as soon as the impetus was lost, and with the cavalry's failure to make the breakthrough quickly into a breakout, the attack was subject to the same bogging down as previous offensives, giving the Germans time to restore their position - or at least contain the British advance - by bringing up reserves. Furthermore, the British themselves lacked the reserves to continue the attack much longer, after their casualties in Flanders and the detachment of troops to the Italian front. Nevertheless, they pressed on, and savage fighting took place in Bourlon Wood, the northernmost limit of the advance. Corporal Henry Gregory, a Machine Gun Corps runner, wrote:

The wood had been like a raging furnace, and it seemed impossible for anything to live in the midst of all that fire, as the shells seemed to cover every inch of the place. The bombardment was as intense at midday as it had been when it started. The roar was deafening, and the screaming, shrieking shells, as they went both ways, made it seem as if there would not be anything or anybody left by the time they had finished.

About 1 p.m. I was called to go with my first dispatch. They could give me no information as to where I could find the Officer that I wanted. A barrage was lying between the two opposing forces, and only open country to go through. This was going to be very dangerous work, and great care would have to be used to get through. I made across country until I got to the end of the road in front of the wood at the left-hand side. I was safe so far, but as I looked on that road it was a blazing, screaming, shell-bursting barrage all the way along, and if ever there was an inferno outside of Hell it was this road. It was one mass of flame the whole length, and I had to go near midway. As the shells came hurtling over, they cut the trees down with a crash. This was an added danger.

But I had to get on somehow. I took my courage in both hands, set my teeth, and made a start on that death-defying journey. As the shells came over, I dodged them as best I could, keeping my eyes open for a falling tree, and dodging from behind one tree to another.

I at last reached my destination. Sad news I received when I got there, as the men told me of the Officers, N.C.O.s, and men who had been killed long before they had reached the wood. Nearly half our company were gone, and the other half must carry on somehow. The Infantry had fared just as badly.

After delivering my dispatch, and getting one to take back telling of the plight they were in, I made my way back along that shell-swept, blazing road once more, always dodging, every nerve strained listening for the shells, and trusting in Providence. I eventually arrived back at Headquarters, and on giving my message to our Commanding Officer, his face turned an ashen grey. The Company in the wood had suffered terrible casualties.

The first day I went up to the wood through this blazing barrage four times, and I was walking hand in hand with death every second of these journeys, I banished fear, and set my mind on getting through each time.

The intense bombardment was kept up all that day and all through the night. We knew now that we were in for the toughest proposition of our lives, and those who came through this trying ordeal must consider themselves lucky. Our men had done that which they had set out to do: that was to get into the wood. The question now was could they hold what they had got with the depleted force? This great struggle was kept up without ceasing for three days and nights.

The second day I made five runs up to the wood with dispatches, each time having to go through the blazing and howling barrage. I had already been up four times on the second day; it was about 9 p.m. and I thought that I had finished for that day. I had taken my boots off, and was making ready for sleep in the cellar, when the Sergeant Major came. He said he was very sorry, but there was another message to go up to the wood. When a Sergeant Major says he is sorry, he means it, for they were not used to throwing needless sympathy about. He detailed another man to go with me; this was always done at night.

We set off at 9 p.m. and it was 6 a.m. next morning when we returned. It was an utter impossibility to get on that road that night; not a flea could have got through the barrage that the enemy put on it. We got through about 4.30 a.m. next morning, when it had quietened down a little, and got back to Headquarters at 6 a.m. It had taken us nine hours to get through and back again; but we were safe, that was everything.

Things were now getting serious in the wood: every [machine-]gun team was considerably reduced, fresh casualties were coming down during the day, and reporting at Headquarters; all Headquarters staff were rounded up and taken up the line to fill the gaps. On the second day here, we had double runners day and night, as it was not considered safe for a runner to go alone...

The men in the wood were having a hard struggle. Rations had not been able to get through. They could not get any sleep or rest. It was attack and counter-attack all the time, and the bombardment was kept up unmercifully.

It was by this time a nightmare of the worst description. At night every little rustle of the trees made the men think the enemy were on top of them, and with missing so much sleep they could hardly keep their eyes open. Each time I went up into the wood the men looked more tired and haggard than on the previous journey. A sharp look-out had to be kept all the time. Some of the men looked a sorry sight: they had not had a meal or a wash since the attack started, and with the constant strain of watching day and night their eyes looked hollow and dim.

On the second afternoon, as I arrived at one of the gun positions, a Sergeant of the Infantry came into our gun position and told us that they had only twenty men left out of his battalion. He was ready to drop for sheer exhaustion. Another N.C.O. came down later the same afternoon, and told us that they had only eighteen men left of their battalion, and that he was the only N.C.O. They were both going down to Headquarters to see if they could get help, as they said they could not hold out much longer.

He told us that the enemy were coming, and they had practically no men in the front line positions. On hearing this, the Officer who was with us, ordered us to fix our bayonets in case they were needed. We had got four machine guns in this position, which had been cut into the side of the road. We waited like grim death for the enemy, ready to fire.

He did not come, as it happened, so after an hour or two, we decided that he was not coming our way.

The third day we were in Bourlon wood was the worst of the lot. The Artillery fire was intensified to such an extent that it was impossible to increase it. The guns boomed all day, the shells screamed and crashed with terrible ferocity, and the road in front of the wood was a road of fire.

I went up from Headquarters seven times on the third and last day we were there, and according to all the rules of warfare I should have been killed or wounded many times over; but my confidence that I should come through all right, never left me during the whole of those terrible experiences.

On this last day, as I went along the road in front of the wood, I had been dodging falling trees and exploding shells all the way, when I came to two tanks which were trying to get out of the way of a German aeroplane which was trying to drop bombs on them. As I was passing these I nearly got trapped as they were turning round, and another danger was the dropping bombs...

I was returning to Headquarters during the afternoon, when I came across the Major commanding our company. He had just returned from the wood; his face was white and drawn with care and worry, for he knew the terrible casualties our men had sustained, in fact, by now our lot were nearly wiped out.

"Well, Gregory," he said, "this is awful, isn't it? "Yes, sir, it is," I replied. We walked on together. He seemed as if he wanted me for company; to be able to talk was a lot in times like these, and these are the times when every station in life is equal. The common danger is apparent to all. We went up the road to Headquarters, talking together. Shells were dropping in the road as we went up, but we got back safely.

We heard after tea that we were being relieved in the wood, after three nights and three days of Hell. When I think of it now, it is a nightmare, even after all these years; that furnace of raging fire where men had to endure. How they lived through it, God only knows.

The Guards were coming up to relieve our men at 11 p.m. that night. One of our Corporals came down to Headquarters to say that the men must be relieved, they could not stand any longer, they had reached the end of their endurance. The Sergeant Major told him that all were being relieved at 11 p.m. that night.

By 22nd November, then, it was obvious that the offensive had not met its objectives and should be broken off. But it continued until the 27th. Byng yielded to pressure from Haig to continue, as had his peers during the Somme and Third Ypres. Haig always disliked changing his objectives, and in late November 1917 he was under great pressure to win a clear victory, for hostility to him in the government had reached such a level that he feared for his job, and therefore his view of how the war should be prosecuted was also in jeopardy. But worse was to follow. The Germans launched a counter-offensive against the overstretched 3rd Army on 30th November and broke through its defences, causing panic and confusion and necessitating a precipitate withdrawal which, by 7th December (when the battle finished) had left the Germans in possession of most of the ground taken on 20th November, 162 guns and several thousand prisoners. Ominously for the future, their success owed much to innovative tactics of using heavily armed 'stormtroops' supported by aircraft to infiltrate the British line, bypassing strongpoints (to be captured later by supporting troops) and accompanied by a crushing hurricane barrage including gas and smoke shells, which was aimed not only at the defences but also at the British lines of communication, so that commanders in the rear had little or no idea of what was going on. Just as ominous for the future was the failure of British corps to coordinate their defensive efforts with their neighbours. And as events were to prove later, the court of inquiry into the debacle, reporting in January 1918, took far more notice of the tactical shortcomings of British troops, especially in the matter of defence in depth, than of the innovations of their opponents. In fairness, however, it was also critical of senior officers for siting their divisions unwisely. Despite its unhappy conclusion, Cambrai had demonstrated the potential of massed tanks as an adjunct to the infantry in an assault. More importantly (in Great War terms), it had also proven the value of predicted artillery fire, and with it, the restoration of surprise to the offensive.

8
Manpower versus Firepower: The March Retreat to the Final Advance

The British commanders had realised by late 1917 that a German offensive in the following spring was likely. With Britain and France tired and short of manpower, American troops only just beginning to arrive in France, Italy in dire straits and Russia out of the war, Germany and her allies held the initiative. This was emphasised by the arrival of an additional 42 German divisions on the Western Front, the bulk of which had been freed for use there by the collapse of Russia. If Germany could break the British and French before the Americans arrived in substantial numbers, the war was won.

The strategic advantage for Germany was reinforced by events in the British camp. After the battles of late 1917, which cost 400,000 British and Colonial casualties, and which only an ardent apologist of Sir Douglas Haig could call unqualified victories (although it is should be noted that they did ultimately contribute to the victory of 1918), Lloyd George and the War Cabinet were determined to exercise closer control than hitherto over strategy. Sir William Robertson, CIGS since 1915, and one of Haig's best allies in London, was forced to resign; GHQ was given a thorough shakeup and Haig's chiefs of staff and intelligence replaced, amongst others. Manpower was more strictly controlled as it was decided to go on the defensive and await the Americans' arrival. The Western Front was given bottom priority for reserves of men, while Haig was forced to take over 25 miles of the French line. This need not have affected the BEF's performance as a fighting force too much, but there was a reluctance in its higher echelons to see it as a mass of firepower, preferring the traditional view of measuring any force's potential effectiveness in terms of 'bayonet strength' - by counting heads. It had not been appreciated that a smaller headcount could attain the same performance if it were provided with the right weapons. More important from the point of view of fighting effectiveness was the decision to reduce the strength of the brigades in

British (though not Colonial) divisions from four to three battalions, in order to bring the remainder up to strength. This was not evenly applied, and some divisions lost as many as six battalions, while others lost none. In all, 145 battalions were broken up and their men transferred to other formations, sometimes not even in the same Army as their old battalion. In a force where group loyalty was primarily directed towards the battalion, and on a lesser scale towards the division, this was terribly disruptive.

In this climate of the assertion of Cabinet power, it may be wondered at that Haig survived in his post. And indeed, he did so only by a whisker. His relations with Lloyd George were at an all time low; curiously, each suspected the other of plotting some kind of coup, and in January 1918, the Prime Minister sent the South African General Smuts to the Front, in order to see whether a replacement for Haig could be found. Fortunately for him, no one outstandingly better was found (or willing to be put forward).

Against this inauspicious background for the BEF, the Germans launched the first of their 1918 offensives, Operation 'Michael', on 21st March. Their new offensive tactics have already been described, at the end of the last chapter. But the scale of this attack was far greater than for the counterstroke at Cambrai. The battering-ram - the artillery - was 6,473 pieces strong, and was supported by 3,532 trench mortars. On the 5th Army front, 43 German divisions attacked 12 British (with two in reserve). Moreover, although the BEF had borrowed from the Germans the tactics of defence in depth, they were not well understood. For example, in some cases outpost positions were dug such that they were not capable of mutual support. Interpretations of the three zone system varied from division to division, which hardly boded well for a consistent system of defence, and the idea of defending strongpoints rather than lines of trenches was entirely foreign to the BEF. Nor were tanks any great benefit, since they were employed thinly spread along the whole front as static strongpoints, rather than as a mobile reserve.[1] These misunderstandings were exacerbated by the fact that 'Michael' fell hardest on 5th Army's part of the line. This was the area recently

---

1   It was at one point proposed that large dugouts be constructed to house these tanks, which would then pop out at a suitable moment, to the discomfiture of the Germans. The Tank Corps referred to this plan as the 'savage rabbits.'

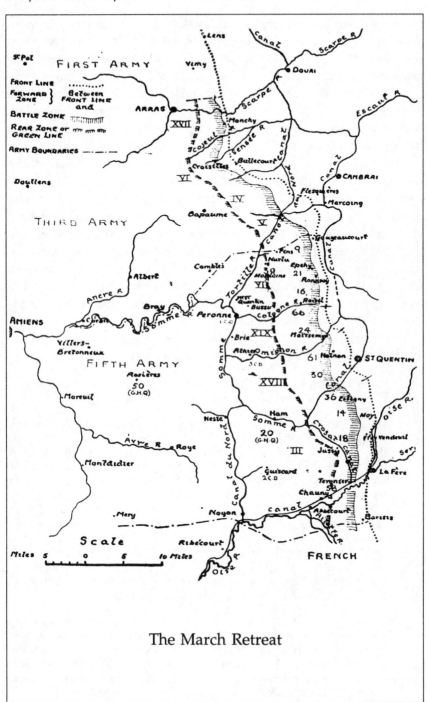

The March Retreat

taken over from the French, and was thinly held by men in poor positions where the third defensive zone had often not yet been prepared. The result was catastrophe, even though the attack was expected. Helped by fog, the Germans surrounded and cut off the outpost positions, and the poor visibility made it difficult for the machine-guns in the battle zone to be effective; out of the eight battalions in XVIII Corps' forward zone, only 50 men in total managed to get back to the battle zone. Still worse, the German policy of bombarding not only defensive positions but also communications rendered the strictly hierarchical command structure of 5th Army completely ineffective. A pattern developed over succeeding days of battalions - or even divisions - being so unsure of what was happening on either side of them that they fell back lest they be outflanked; this then led to the flanks of neighbouring formations being exposed, forcing them to retire in a similarly uncoordinated manner. Counter-attacks - vital to the three zone defensive system - were out of the question as corps, division and even brigade commanders simply did not know where their men were.

The ubiquitous Lt. Col. Fraser-Tytler (then a major), returning from leave on 23rd March, recounted his impressions:

> ...the 19th Corps foretold the exact day, hour and minute of the German Zero hour, and many other predictions were as exactly right.
>
> I think one of the chief factors was the dense morning mist of the 21st and 22nd; it blinded every gun, M.G. and rifle on the front, and beside this the mist upset all the carefully made plans of our Artillery Commanders. Their pre-arranged counter-preparation barrages, which were planned to search out all the likely assembly points from which the enemy could launch his infantry after the preliminary bombardment was over, all came to naught. As it turned out, practically all communications with the front line were cut by the opening barrage, and in many cases the infantry imagined that they were being attacked hours before it really happened, so S.O.S. messages were sent back to the Artillery, compelling them to cease their all-important counter-preparation work and to drop their fire back into No Man's Land where, for the time being, every shell was wasted.
>
> It is a well-known fact that if you have time to study closely a fixed barrage across a certain area, it is always possible to detect the weakest parts in it. In some cases the Hun must have been able to watch this barrage for three or four hours before the scheduled hour of the attack, and in consequence probably got through without heavy casualties, and moreover had not been shaken by our shelling of his assembly points.

The speed of the Hun attack was extraordinary. He certainly advanced twice as quickly as we ever did... and with his irresistible numbers was able to ignore and leave behind him any specially stubborn strong points which did not yield to his first onslaught. The result of this speed was that our men, retreating from the front system, had no time to settle down in the second line of defence before the Hun was on top of them. These are only the rough ideas which struck one at the moment. Doubtless hereafter endless bitter controversies will rage over the rights and wrongs of this retreat...

Looking at the horses, sorting out one's kit for war once more, and routing up the forgotten "battle bowler" [i.e. steel helmet], occupied the evening [of 24th March], and early next day we started off in a lorry for Abbeville. We meant to go by train to Amiens, but the railway station did not look inviting or progressive, and no one knew "nothing more about no trains nowhere." Hence we were driven to call on the A.Q.M.G. and M.T.O.C. and many other worthies, and by assuring them that the War could not possibly be waged successfully unless we reached Army Head-Quarters at once, we got permission to take the lorry as far as Amiens. Needless to add, it required much persuasion, since the breath of war had not yet ruffled the officialdom of Abbeville.

On reaching Amiens soon after midday, we found the town packed with people looking for their units, and as the lorry refused to move a yard further, we dumped our servants and kit in a bedroom at the Hotel du Rhin. After an exciting hunt I managed to snaffle a Ford car from a Y.M.C.A. hut into which Hills, Diggle (B.M., 21st Division R.A.) and I packed ourselves and fled to Villers Brettoneux. There we found in the Chateau the Fifth Army Head-Quarters after their fourth move since the attack.

Standing outside I met General Gough as cheery as ever, but rather scornful at our late arrival for the picnic. The Chateau walls were covered with the usual maze of telephone wires which Signals had erected in wonderfully quick time, and inside the Chateau were many vast empty rooms in which the various branches [of the Army staff] were working.

Having found R.A. we got our orders from Col. Broad. Briefly they were to look after the area between the Somme and the River Luce, to organize it as regards rations, catching stragglers, helping the siting of fresh batteries coming up, and a hundred and one other duties. We then collected a car and several riding horses, and divided up the [Army training] school officers and N.C.O.'s between our show and the R.A. Rest Camp. The latter was being run by Waite, the School Adjutant, who was in charge of all the lost R.A. personnel. We had a busy night of it, as movements from point to point were much hindered by the seething mass of retreating traffic.

On the previous night Huns, disguised as British officers on motor cycles, had got through into the back areas. They caused one or two serious panics by ordering villagers to clear out at once, shouting that the Hun Cavalry was at hand. As may be imagined, when once a mass of motor lorries starts stampeding down a road it is not the easiest matter in the world to check them, especially when the darkness is such that it may be felt. So at several cross-roads we posted picquets with a lorry or caterpillar [tractor] beside them to be ready in case a motor vehicle panic started to block the road and thus check the panic effectively though perhaps somewhat abruptly.

Some staff officer asked one of my picquets what orders I had given them. The N.C.O. replied: "The Major said we were just to shoot everybody making alarm or spreading despondency, and most particularly to shoot officers." Some were shot, but life was too busy to go into further details.

Late that evening (25th) the Army Head-Quarters moved back to Dury, and the general position of the front seemed more threatening than ever. Just before dawn I motored forward to the great La Flaque Dump to hurry on the evacuation or destruction of its contents. It was a vast dump covering acres of ground, the R.E. portion of it, chiefly timber and iron, had, of course, to be left, but the gun park, I.O.M. works and ordnance stores were nearly cleared, and the ration dump was reduced to 50,000 rations instead of the million or so usually there. I tried to hasten the clearance of the gun park, but the labour company men who were loading the lorries were nearly dead beat. There was also 10,000 gallons of aeroplane petrol A. We took as much as we could for our own private lorries, as it almost doubles their speed, but I fear the bulk of this dump had later to be set on fire.

On returning to Villers Brettoneux I found that the 19th Corps Head-Quarters (very old friends) had just moved into the Chateau. As the morning wore on things began to get more hectic than ever, as it became impossible to keep in touch with the flank Divisions or Corps. We were very busy all day with all sorts of work, chiefly collecting rifles, S.A.A. or lorries, forming stragglers into digging parties or companies for defence, finding lost batteries or guns, anything from 9.2" Howitzers to 18-pdrs., and getting them into action to shoot point blank down roads. These and numerous other details involved much motoring and telephoning to find various mislaid units, from an Army Corps downwards.

It is difficult to give a description of the hopeless jumble of such a day or the quaint mixture of scenes witnessed on the main road. A torrent of traffic, thousands of refugees, in most cases pushing their worldly goods in a wheelbarrow, a pathetic stream it was, chiefly composed of very old and very young people, ever flowing westward.

In the garden beside me two small girls in clean pinafores played shuttlecock in the bright March sunshine, while just over the road stood a deserted handcart, with a very old woman strapped upon it, dead and abandoned. On the other side of the road we were getting an 8-inch Howitzer into action to shoot down the straight road into Warfussee, and near it a company of our lost gunners were making a stockade for the future blocking of the road.

Late that afternoon we received orders from Army to move back to Longeau, an eastern suburb of Amiens, taking with us all the personnel of the R.A. Rest Camp and to join forces with Colonel Davidson, who had moved his gun park back there...

[The next day] At the R.A. Office I heard that the gun park was to be cleared out of Longeau and moved back to Nampes, about twenty miles further West. An army gun park, however, even in peaceful times, is not a very mobile thing. Including damaged, new or repaired guns we had at Longeau some ninety 18-pdrs., forty 4.5 Howitzers, twenty 6-inch, a few 8-inch, large morsels of 9.2 Howitzers, several thousand Lewis and Vickers machine-guns, about two train-loads of stores, spare parts, machine-gun drums, belts etc., and complete workshops of various grades, medium, light, and heavy. Hitherto, of course, no artillery officer had ever been allowed to breathe the sacred atmosphere surrounding the departments under the control of the Ordnance Services, but in this crisis, for certain reasons which I will not put on paper, Army had decided to give absolute plenipotentiary powers to R.A. officers throughout the whole branch, hence the Colonel's job, which after two days, fell to my lot. It was a curious position, as one had to deal with several Ordnance Colonels.

Having got my orders at Amiens I whirled round various villages collecting 120 horse-power caterpillars, four-wheel drives, and lorries from various super-heavy Howitzer batteries which had managed to escape, or which had not been in action at all. All this mixed pack of vehicles I sent racing down the road (if a caterpillar can be said to race at two miles an hour) all the way to Longeau. I also collected many lost and wandering lorries and about 200 equally lost Labour Company men with a few officers, and they, too, were sent to work in our vineyard.

Then on to Nampes to select the site of the gun park, but seven casualty clearing stations had got there before us, and the station was filled with 4,000 walking wounded, so Nampes was impossible. Having inspected various other stations on that branch line, I went back to Army to see General Hambre [DA and QMG; actually named Hambro] and Colonel Craik (Transportation) and it was decided that the gun park should move to Poix. On my return to Longeau I found that the bulk of the carts and lorries had arrived and that during the day Spragge and the others had managed to dispose of a lot of new guns to batteries applying for them; they also got rid of a thousand Lewis guns.

We now started evacuating in earnest; long strings of guns were tied behind each "cat." and a party of walking men were detailed to help to guide the tail round corners in the road. One or two guns were also tied behind each loaded lorry, and the whole lot were sent off that evening on their 26-mile march to Poix. An engine being luckily available at Amiens station, a heavily-loaded train with one of my officers and a hundred men in it was sent off forthwith, so that the shop at Poix might be opened straight away.

Before dark I tried to get some faint idea of what my ever-changing commando really did consist of. I found I should have 5 officers and 6 N.C.O. school instructors, all of whom could be relied on to apply the necessary hustle and ginger to the remainder. The latter consisted of a fluctuating quantity of labour men, perhaps 300 in all, with four officers, a lost trench-mortar battery with three officers and some men, the ordnance staff, some light workshops, and an unknown quantity of vehicles, which, with about three acres of ground covered with stores and guns, completed my flock. One can never trust the stray vehicles very far, as, should they come across their own unit, they usually bolt off and rejoin, never to be heard of again by us.

The bombing of the previous night had hastened the evacuation of Amiens by the civil population, and as we had no wish to repeat our experiences [Fraser-Tytler had also been bombed], we moved our kits into a very comfortable deserted villa, in the garden of which were hens, and still better, plenty of eggs... I enjoyed here the first real meal and the first sleep of any sort I had had since I left the school three days before.

The evacuation of the gun park continued all the next day, which was the 28th. A very long train loaded with equipment of every sort turned up at our station, where it was certainly not wanted, but we managed to increase its load with a good many tons of our stores, and it was sent off to find its way to Poix. It was a busy day; endless batteries poured in asking for everything under the sun; men and horses were the only things we could supply easily, as Waite had plenty of them corralled in his rest camp. We reduced paper work and signing to a minimum, so batteries could come in and get new guns, stores, horses and men, and be off again in a few hours.

On calling at Army Head-Quarters before noon I found that our General had gone, thanks to the black hand of political influence, and that the Fourth Army was taking over. The afternoon was indeed a busy one, trying to get everything away and at the same time keep back enough to supply the wants of our many customers. As we have stores of every sort of guns, from 13-pdrs. to 12-inch Howitzers, you can imagine the complexity of these acres of stores. We had the luck, however, to catch another railway engine, and with the help of many trucks got another big train-load away that night, which greatly cleared the congestion.

In the course of Operation 'Michael,' the Germans advanced 40 miles, inflicted 178,000 casualties on the British and captured or destroyed 1,000 guns. The crisis of the battle arose when the remnants of 5th Army were in danger of losing touch altogether with 3rd Army to their left and the French 6th Army to their right. Loss of contact with the French posed the greater threat, for if the Germans could force themselves between the French and British armies, there was a risk that the British would fall back to their bases on the coast, exposing the French to defeat on their own. The situation was plainly desperate, and in an attempt to ensure greater Franco-British cooperation and an overall control of strategy and strategic reserves, General Foch of the French army was appointed supreme commander of all the Allied armies. Haig's objections to this before the German offensive were overcome by fear of defeat and his suspicions as to the intentions of ther French C-in-C, General Pétain, and at the Doullens conference of 26th March, it was he who proposed Foch's appointment.

On 6th April, the German advance was finally halted. This was owing to a number of factors. One was that 5th Army (by now re-designated as 4th Army, as Rawlinson replaced the 'degummed' Gough) had retired to better defensive positions; another that, as so often with attacking troops, the Germans simply lost their momentum. Notwithstanding the effectiveness of stormtroop tactics, as the offensive progressed, attacks were all too frequently made in traditional, massed formations and casualties were very heavy. On 28th March, the main German attack was against 1st and 3rd Armies near Arras; it was contained with little loss of ground:

> The initial bombardment had been carried out with an enormous concentration of guns of every conceivable size, gas-shells being scattered about profusely, especially among the batteries - as we had assumed. As for the forward posts, they were subjected for hours to a terrifying bombardment from trench-mortars, minenwerfer and high explosive which must have almost blotted them out before any advance was attempted. Two of our companies must have been exterminated, but, doubtless, some of the men were prisoners. At any rate, they were overrun and masses of Germans, all wearing packs (also, it afterwards transpired, carrying six days' supplies and extra boots), stormed onwards and entered into a desperate fight for Marine Trench where H.Q. had been. It was finally necessary to retire to the battle zone (Red Line) where orders were given that it must be held at all costs. For the rest of the day, the remainder of the L.R.B.[London Rifle Brigade] with the Westminsters on one side of them had fired continuously on the

masses of Germans that came on against them, and the ground before
the trench was thickly strewn with dead. So confident were the enemy
that they would break through that about 9a.m. a German battery had
been seen beyond Gavrelle, drawn up on the road ready to gallop
forward: our artillery had promptly directed fire on it and made a nice
mess of things. "It's the finest day in the history of the regiment," said
the sergeant. "There's not many of 'em left, but they've killed simply
thousands with bombs and rifle-fire and Lewis guns. Fritz hadn't got a
kick left in him." [Rfmn. Aubrey Smith]

Unlike British attacking troops, all of whom applied infiltration tactics,
the stormtroops were especially combed out from the rest of the army.
This lowered the quality of the follow-up divisions, and they were not
trained in the new tactics - hence their old-fashioned, massed
formations. And they could not be protected by a creeping barrage, for
the German gunners never mastered the technique. The hurricane
bombardment of 21st March was extremely intense, but not technically
subtle. In addition, the troops became exhausted after so much fighting
and marching, and it has been suggested that their morale suffered
when they came across the immense dumps of stores of all kinds
abandoned by the retreating British, contrasting so sharply as they did
with what was available to them and the German civilian population
after over three years of naval blockade. Some of Aubrey Smith's
comrades had been captured, but escaped, and told him of the lengths
to which the Germans were driven:

> They had been sent with a party of others to clear the old battlefield
> near Bourlon Wood and testified to the avidity with which the enemy
> salved everything they could lay their fingers on. Our boys had nothing
> but a plate of mangel-wurzel or turnip soup, a piece of bread and some
> coffee for their entire day's meal, but the Germans fed the prisoners
> badly partly because they were so hard up for food themselves. They
> even dug up the old British cook-houses and made use of the decaying
> food they discovered there, in order to feed the hundred thousand odd
> prisoners they had recently taken.

Perhaps crucially, they also made a serious tactical mistake in having
no mobile arm of exploitation. The German High Command had no
faith in tanks (although a few captured from the British were used by
the Germans in 1918), even after Cambrai, and had long since retrained
their cavalry as infantry. The reliance of their attack on 'footslogging'
left them unable to exploit the undoubted chaos in 5th Army during the
first few days of the offensive.

However, the end of Operation 'Michael' was by no means the end
of German attacks in 1918. The next blow against the BEF was on the

River Lys, in Flanders on 9th April, with the intention of taking the Channel Ports. This attack - codenamed 'Georgette'[2] - also enjoyed initial success, along a 20 mile front running south from Ypres. Many of the British troops there were not fresh, having been moved up from the Somme for a rest after the fighting in March, and the collapse of three Portuguese brigades left a large hole in the line. While a number of important towns were lost, and the territorial gains of Third Ypres abandoned, the Germans failed to capture the vital rail junction of Hazebrouck and after nine days the offensive petered out. At this point some British observers noted a lowering of German troops' morale as compared to when they were attacking in March. A tendency for them to stop fighting to loot captured stores was perceived even by the German High Command, and it seemed that officers and NCOs did not feel sufficiently sure of their authority to prevent this. Nevertheless, their attacks continued.

The next 'push' (on 27th May) took place against largely French forces on the Chemin des Dames, near the River Aisne and the scene of much bitter fighting earlier in the war. Its limited function was to draw Allied reserves away from Flanders, in preparation for another attack there. In the event, the commander in the area, General Duchesne adopted old fashioned defensive tactics, manning his front line very strongly, against the protests of British commanders under him who were all too aware of the power of a hurricane barrage as employed in 'Michael.' The unfortunate machine-gunner, Corporal Henry Gregory, was in the front line:

> We had blown the candles out and were in the dark, when all at once a terrific bombardment opened out. What a deafening noise! I had been in some bombardments before, but this beat the lot.
>
> One of the sentries came to the top of the dug-out steps and shouted, "Stand to!" He shouted at the top of his voice, but it seemed like a faint, unearthly voice, and we could only make it out as a whisper, for the noise of the bombardment drowned everything else. The voice sounded weird and uncanny, as if it came from some unnatural being; it was a voice of fear and terror.
>
> The shells were now coming over like hail, and bursting all over the

---

2   It had originally been codenamed 'George,' but was renamed because it was smaller than originally envisaged, owing to the casualties suffered in 'Michael.'

trenches. On hearing the voice, we all struggled off our beds, found and lit a few candles, quickly put on our equipment, which we had left ready, and grabbed our rifles. We then ran up the dug-out steps and to our positions at the guns.

The guns were now both blazing away 600 rounds a minute. In a few minutes the water in the casing of the guns was boiling. We brought as much ammunition as we could, and were all prepared to do our best. All had their allotted duties: some to fill belts with bullets, one to fire the gun, and another to see that the belt went through the gun straight. If there were any stoppages, this man had to put matters right. We were blazing away as fast as the guns would go.

The shells that were coming over were blowing the trenches down all around us. Jerry now sent over a lot of "Flying Pigs," as we called them. These were trench mortars; when in the air they had a tail of fire, and were the shape of a pig. He sent hundreds of these over, and as they exploded they went off with a deafening crash. The screaming, whistling shells, and the swish, swish of the machine gun bullets as they came our way, made us realize that we were in for a rough handling.

When the enemy spotted the fire of our two guns, my God, how he did smash at us! He smashed, and smashed, and smashed, with every kind of shell that it was possible to send over. He nearly blew the position to pieces.

I had been into the dug-out for more ammunition. When I was returning a shell burst right into the gun position that I was feeding. It blew everything sky high. I made a dash back, and a shower of earth came toppling on top of us. Both the guns were now out of action; one had been hit and wrecked, and it was impossible to get near the other, as Jerry was pounding away with shells for all he was worth.

The sky was now alight with the flashes of the guns, and the explosions of the shells and trench mortars. The stink of the powder was choking. The trenches were practically levelled, and if you wanted to speak to someone only a foot away, you had to shout at the top of your voice, and then it was only like a whisper, for the noise was deafening...

We took what cover we could, crouched down by the trench by the dug-out steps. We were now expecting that every minute the enemy would be over with the bayonet. We had our bayonets fixed as a last resort, eight of us all told, and we had not seen anyone else since the action started. Bombs were dished out, and we were to defend the positions as best we could.

While waiting, we heard somebody coming down the trench. We thought that it must be the enemy, and got our bombs ready to throw; but on turning the bend of the trench about ten yards away, we saw it was a Tommy.

When he got to us, he told us that all the Infantry had been wiped out in the bombardment. How anything could possibly live through it was incredible. The man was in a terrible state of terror and exhaustion; he looked as if he would drop any minute. He was pitiful to look at, just on the point of shell shock. His face was pinched and drawn, such a haggard, weary look; he could not keep the flesh on his face still, and his teeth were chattering...

In about another five minutes we heard more footsteps coming down the trench. We waited with our bombs, as before. This turned out to be another of our Infantry, and he also was ordered to stay with us. These two Infantrymen were the only ones we saw during all that night and morning. There were now ten of us all told. This second man was in just the same state of physical exhaustion as the first...

We were all watching for the trench mortars that were flying through the sky. These burst with a terrible crash, as if the world were falling to pieces. By this time the trenches were practically levelled... After they had pounded us like this for two and a half hours, they threw gas shells over for another half an hour. We had now to put on our gas masks...

The bombardment now quietened down a little. What was going to happen now? Just as we were wondering this, a swarm of large rats came squeaking and squealing from the two dug-outs. They were running on top of what was left of the parapet. First one and then another was gassed. The fumes hung thick everywhere. One could not see for it. We still had our gas masks on...

It was now breaking day. We looked over what was left of our parapet, and saw the enemy advancing in droves. They were coming across No Man's Land. There were now eight of us, and we decided that we would try to get back to Headquarters in the line. We went down the trench, until we came to a wide gap where the trench was completely down for about nine yards.

We looked round the end to see where the enemy had got to, and saw a machine gun in position in the field, waiting for us to pass the gap. We were trapped...

The degree of success enjoyed by the Germans surprised even them. As a result, Ludendorff, their commander in chief (in fact though not name) lost sight of the limited nature of the operation and poured more men and guns into it, who after two days had advanced to within fifty miles of Paris. However, they were in a narrow salient, and so he ordered further attacks to enlarge it. His reserve, the *18th Army*, was put into the battle on 9th June, but even it was held by the French, after some initial success. On 11th June the attack was stopped, and still with a later offensive in Flanders in mind, Ludendorff ordered attempts to be made (in mid-July) to break through the French line at its weakest points, east and west of Reims. The intention was to threaten Paris, but only the western attack enjoyed a degree of success, establishing a bridgehead across the River Marne. But now the Germans had expended all their reserves, while the Allies had been reinforced by 15 American divisions, each twice as strong as one in a European army. The initiative now passed back to them.

The first counterstroke against the Germans, in the Second Battle of the Marne, was launched on 18th July by the French and Americans. As was now commonplace, no preliminary bombardment gave the surprise away. The German line collapsed and they were pushed back to the Aisne over the next two weeks.

Then the British, using the Australian, Canadian and III Corps, attacked on a 19,000 yard front near Amiens on 8th August. Sir Henry Rawlinson, in command of the 1916 Somme offensive, was responsible for the attack. Secrecy beforehand was strictly maintained, even to the extent of the Canadian Corps moving its wireless units to the 2nd Army sector when it moved to the Somme, for the discovery of its presence would have certainly disclosed to the Germans that an attack was imminent. By this time, the Australian and Canadian Corps were the strongest formations left to the BEF, still having 12-battalion divisions, and in the latter case, not having been involved in the fighting of March and April.

Like the French on the Marne, the 4th Army troops used tanks, but in unprecedented numbers - a total of 580, including supply tanks and 50 of the new Mark V* model[3], an infantry-carrying modification of the Mark V now in service. The latter was a great improvement on the Mark IV, having a more powerful and reliable engine, a maximum speed of 4.6 miles per hour and much better gearing (which made fewer demands on the crew). However, ventilation was worse than in previous models, and the radiator was mounted inside the tank, with the result that often the crew's endurance failed before the machine's. Seventy-two were the new Medium Mark A, rather misleadingly called the 'Whippet;' this was a smaller tank than the Mark V, had a top

---

3   These were not in fact a success, the infantry inside being overcome by heat and
        fumes.

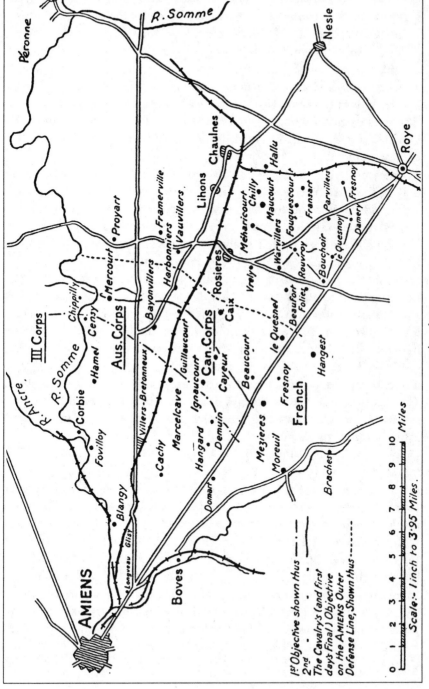

speed of 8.3 miles per hour and was armed with four machine-guns. It was designed for exploitation, in conjunction with the cavalry.

In addition to the artillery providing the barrage (once again, predicted fire was employed), field guns were to act in close support of the infantry. Rawlinson also followed the advice of the French General Mangin, who had played a major part in their victory on the Marne, and had his reserves move up at the same time as the first attackers; in this semi-open warfare, the first wave could be expected to move on quickly, and this was an attack in depth. Experience at Cambrai had demonstrated that by the time they had captured the first objective, troops were too tired to be effective. At Amiens the attackers were to halt at the first objective, and the reserves would 'leap-frog' through them and carry on to the next, and so on. Waves were not used; the troops advanced in depth in small, well spaced columns, in diamond-shaped groups; if shelled, these would scatter. Mortars and heavy machine guns were to move up with the infantry, in order to assist in the reduction of strongpoints and machine-gun posts. Most importantly, the attackers were instructed to press on, and not worry about their flanks; unsuppressed positions there could be dealt with by the reserves. In this way, the momentum of the assault was to be maintained; all too often in trench warfare worries about being outflanked had led successful attacks not to be exploited. Rawlinson also had 800 aeroplanes at his disposal, including a number of bombers. These carried out contact patrols, dropped supplies to the infantry and harassed the Germans with machine-gun fire and bombs, beyond artillery range where necessary.

At 4.20a.m. the barrage, from 2,000 guns and howitzers, opened. The infantry and tanks were, like the Germans on 21st March, helped by mist, and the effect on German morale of hundreds of tanks emerging from the latter was considerable. Despite some problems - III Corps, on the left, had the most difficult ground and most alert enemy to deal with, and so was delayed - the attack was a great success. Even though the first waves of infantry soon left the mortars and Vickers guns behind, they dealt with strongpoints through the well-established techniques of using Lewis guns and grenades, while other troops worked round the flanks. It was noted that the German positions were poorly dug and wired, despite an abundance of entrenching tools and barbed wire, another sign of failing morale. On the first day the Germans were pushed back 12,000 yards, losing over 26,000 men (of whom two-thirds had surrendered) and 400 guns, not to mention trench mortars, machine guns and other material. It was the greatest defeat suffered by the German army in the war to date. Major W.H.L. Watson observed events on the right flank, where the Australian Corps was:

> We moved forward unobtrusively... to an inconspicuous knoll. There we lay in comfort, watching the farther advance of the Australians. The country was quite open and bare, though broken with unexpected valleys. A slight breeze had swept away the mist, and the morning was bright and sunny. A few hundred yards in front of us, the Australians were walking forward nonchalantly, led by a score of tanks. Occasionally a shell would fall among them and they would scatter momentarily, but it was rarely that a man was left upon the ground. From the valley beyond, which we could not see, came the rattle of Lewis guns, and once or twice bursts from the enemy machine-guns. To the left and behind us our field-guns, drawn up in the open, were firing for dear life, and away to the right along a slight dip a battery of field-guns was trotting forward. Overhead the sky was loud with the noise of our aeroplanes, some flying low above the battle and others glistening in the sun high among the clouds.
>
> The Australians disappeared with the tanks over the skyline, and the supporting infantry in little scattered bodies passed us, marching forward cheerily over the rough grass. We were already three miles within the enemy defences.
>
> We pressed on northwards to the Cerisy Valley, which we knew had been full of German field-guns... Our gunners had done their work with terrible thoroughness. The bottom of the valley was so broken with shell-holes that it was barely possible to drive a limber between them. Four or five of the enemy guns remained desolate among a wild confusion of shattered waggons and dead horses.

By 13th August, the advance had slowed, and was approaching the wilderness of the old Somme battlefield. Rawlinson realised, after some prodding from the commander of the Canadian Corps, Sir Arthur Currie, that further fighting would at best yield limited returns, and that there was a real possibility of failure. With the eyes of the politicians upon them, 1918 was not the time for generals to incur pointlessly heavy casualties. Rawlinson persuaded Haig that the battle be broken off. For the first time, Haig agreed, despite being under pressure from Foch not to do so.

The victory at Amiens rested on a number of factors, over and above those which had permitted the initial success at Cambrai. Firstly, Rawlinson had realised that firepower was the key to success, and took care to maximise that available to the infantry, not least because, by August 1918, a division contained about half as many combat troops as in 1916. Secondly, it was now routine for artillery commanders to calculate the weight of shell required to provide an adequate barrage and bombardment (this process had evolved in the course of the previous year), so the blind faith of July 1916 had been replaced by a precise, mathematical approach. Thirdly, there was now an abundant supply of artillery pieces and ammunition; the munitions industry had not only replaced the losses of March, but increased the BEF's complement of artillery. Fourthly, this meant that not only were the demands of the barrage on the field artillery met (about 700 guns fired 350,000 shells on 8th August), but there was enough heavy artillery to undertake a comprehensive and crushing counter-battery programme. And fifthly, infantry tactics and infantry-tank co-operation were sufficiently well-developed to minimise casualties and to subdue German strongpoints with relative ease, given the artillery support to let them get forward.

Why, then, did the offensive stop? Apart from the arrival of German reinforcements, which was of less significance than earlier in the war, owing to their poor morale, the principal reason was that it took time to organise another attack like that on the first day. Artillery targets had to be identified, and the sound-ranging and aerial photography required for this took time. Furthermore, the guns and howitzers had then to be ranged on these. The infantrymen were tired, and no substantial reinforcements were available. Tank crews were even more tired, and in any case, there was a high rate of attrition amongst the tanks themselves. Although a large number could be salvaged, the process was not fast.

From now on, the Allied strategy was one of giving the Germans no respite from attacks all along the line; no time to rest their troops and none to muster reserves. If an attack bogged down, another would be launched elsewhere, ensuring that only success was reinforced and that the Germans would have to fall back - even when not attacked - for fear of being outflanked as a result of Allied success elsewhere. After Amiens, 3rd Army, to the north of 4th, attacked; then 1st Army, on the left of the former did so. During the latter operations, the Canadians broke through the Drocourt-Quéant switch. This move outflanked the 'Winter Line,' on which the Germans had hoped to make a stand for the rest of the year, and their High Command was compelled on 2nd

September to order a withdrawal to the Hindenburg Line. In addition, the area gained in April, to the north, was abandoned. Fourth Army recommenced its attacks on 23rd August and the French and Americans were also attacking further south. As the Germans were pushed back, their infantry generally showed further signs of diminishing morale, although the backbone of the continued resistance, the machine-gunners, did not. However, even fresh divisions were proving unable to withstand well-organised British attacks; the weapon systems used in the latter were too strong to withstand, although it is arguable whether tanks were used as fully as they might have been.

By 11th September, the Germans had reached the Hindenburg Line, and were almost back to where they had started from on 21st March. This formidable obstacle had been strengthened in the time since the Germans first pulled back to it, in March 1917. Now it consisted of six defensive lines, a total of 6,000 yards deep, protected by belts of wire hundreds of yards deep and liberally sprinkled with pillboxes, machine-gun posts and concrete shelters for the defenders. The first three of the six lines were the old British reserve, main and outpost lines; these were not viewed as being a serious obstacle. Then came the advanced Hindenburg system, which, although originally an outpost line, had been substantially strengthened, and would present problems for the attackers. The main Hindenburg system would be an even tougher nut to crack, with the defence system based round the Canal du Nord in the north, and the St. Quentin canal in the south. The first of these, though incomplete when the war broke out, was 30 to 40 yards wide and in a cutting 30 to 40 feet deep. It was largely dry, but protected by three strong trench lines. The St. Quentin canal was in a cutting with steep banks, 50 feet deep, was 35 feet wide and held mud or water to a depth of at least six feet. Belts of wire were laid on the banks and in the water, and machine-guns were emplaced to provide flanking fire. Canal tunnels at le Tronquoy and Bellicourt were converted into shelters for hundreds of men, and although the canal itself was obviously not difficult to cross at these points, additional trench lines had been constructed to guard them. Lastly, there was the reserve Hindenburg system; this was incomplete, and it was hoped that it could be taken on the same day as the main system.

As their troops pursued the retreating Germans, Rawlinson, Byng and Haig consulted one another regarding the way in which to proceed. All were agreed that the attack on the main Hindenburg system must be preceded by the seizure of the old British lines and the advanced system; the Germans were to be afforded as little respite as possible, in order that their morale not be given the chance to recover. Third Army launched its attack on 12th September, against the Trescault and Havrincourt spurs, in the southern part of the old Cambrai battlefield. On a five mile front, an advance of nearly a mile was achieved, against stubborn resistance. Havrincourt village, inside the advanced Hindenburg system, was captured. On 18th September, 4th Army made its attack; this was a set-piece operation, with limited objectives. Although only partial success was achieved on the flanks, in the centre the Australians took all three old British lines and broke into the advanced system. Their 6,800 infantry (consisting of only about 400 men per battalion) took over 4,000 prisoners and 76 guns, while advancing 5,000 yards on a four mile front. In the next few days, III and IX Corps, on the Australians' flanks, pushed forward. By 26th September, 1st, 3rd and 4th Armies faced the main system. Between 8th August and the former date (50 days), the 1st, 3rd and 4th Armies had advanced 25 miles on a 40 mile front, taking about 180,000 casualties. In 1916, it had taken four and a half months to advance eight miles on a 12 mile front, and cost 420,000 casualties.

The assault on the Canal du Nord took place on 27th September. First and 3rd Armies made the attack, with the Canadian Corps (1st Army) forming the spearhead. After careful reconnaissance, it attacked on a narrow front, the (risky) plan being to fan out to a front of six miles once the defences had been breached. An unusually heavy creeping barrage was employed, with five zones, and on the first day the Canadians gained or even passed all their objectives. The rest of 1st Army's attackers and 3rd Army's met with less success, but by the end of 28th September, a breach twelve miles wide and six deep had been made in the German defences. However, as at Amiens, gains diminished with time and the inability of the artillery to keep up with the infantry's advance, and unlike the latter battle, German resistance was stiff. The offensive was stopped after 1st October.

Meanwhile, on 28th September, 2nd Army, which together with the Belgian Army and French troops, formed an army group under the command of the King of the Belgians, began the offensive in Flanders. On the first day an advance of four to six and a half miles was made, even though it was across the wasteland created during Third Ypres. The next day, the Belgians recaptured Passchendaele village, or rather, its site; it had been levelled by shellfire in 1917. However, the weather broke on the 29th, and boggy conditions returned to the area; again the artillery could not keep up with the infantry and so, on 2nd October, the offensive was stopped while the former caught up. The Germans had brought up enough reserves to make further advance too costly without proper artillery support.

4th Army resumed its offensive on 29th September, against the southern portion of the main Hindenburg position. Although its troops, especially in the Australian and III Corps, were tired, they were reinforced by two fresh American divisions. And Rawlinson and his subordinates enjoyed two advantages when planning the battle. The first of these was that at Amiens, the Australians had captured precise plans of this sector of the Hindenburg Line, even down to the positions of individual batteries and observation posts. And the second was that owing to their fondness for the canal as an obstacle, the Germans had put this system in a valley, with the advanced system on the ridge above. Now that the latter had been captured, the attackers enjoyed superb observation over the main system. This meant that surprise was not necessary. Normally, if they were alerted to an impending attack, the Germans would move their artillery in order to make counter-battery fire less efficacious, and bring up reserves of infantry. But under the circumstances prevailing here, any such actions could be spotted easily by the attackers' artillery observers, and they could simply order the necessary adjustments to the gunners' aim. The British, Australians and Americans attacked on a 10,000 yard front, with over 160 tanks, after a two day preliminary bombardment which was over twice as heavy as that delivered at Amiens. This was the heaviest the BEF's artillery delivered in the war; for example, 945,052 shells were fired between midday on 28th and midday on 29th September. It also contained the surprise element that 30,000 of the shells contained mustard gas, which had not been used before by the BEF. Partly because of the inexperience of the Americans, whose poor mopping-up led to heavy casualties in the Australians following them, the northern flank of the attack, in the tunnel sector, was held up, but in the south the defences were breached to a depth of 6,000 yards by the 46th Division (in IX Corps), which had most ingeniously improvised rafts and the like for crossing the canal, and to whom 3,000 lifebelts from Channel steamers had been issued. The by now well-tried formula of the combination of tanks, infantry and artillery had

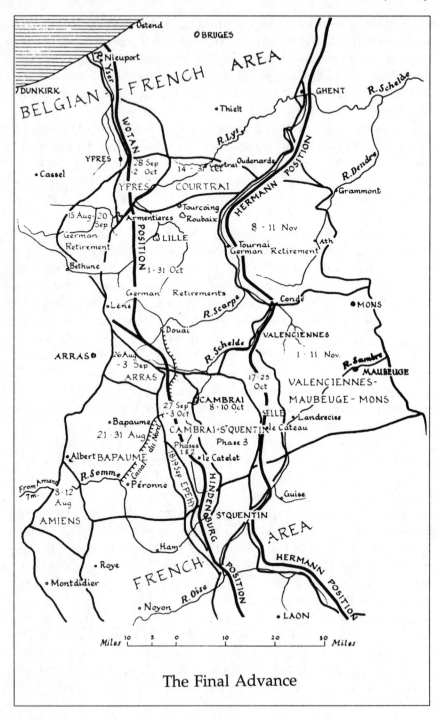

The Final Advance

breached the strongest defensive systems on the Western Front. In the course of the next six days, the main Hindenburg system was overrun to the same depth on a width of 11,000 yards. This was greatly assisted by a lack of substantial reserves for the Germans; the Allies were by now attacking on a 100 mile front, and the defenders had to make do with weak, local resources. Haig's optimism of 1916 and 1917 finally appeared to be justified; the Germans were overstretched and beginning to collapse. Nevertheless, they were still capable of resistance. Lt. T. Lloyd, 15th Cheshires, was in action on 21st October:

> Stretching across fields of swedes and stubble, the thin line of khaki figures, a mile long, moved steadily forward. Never did the colour of dress blend better with that of nature. There were no guns to afford protective fire, so we fired round after round from rifles held at the hips to create a mild barrage of our own. Bullets came from all angles to thickly spray the ground lying immediately before us, and a constant rattle in the direction of the Sweveghem road, together with numerous bursts from the farms in front, showed only too vividly the strength of "Jerry's" resources. We caught many glimpses of Germans disappearing into the folds of the undulating ground ahead. Still, they were showing wonderful resources in fighting a rearguard action. A distant [machine-]gun would give covering fire until the one on the line of resistance had withdrawn to a position well in the rear. Then this weapon in turn would cover the retreat of the other, and so on by a series of movements or relays affecting numerous Maxims, capture was avoided, as well as affording a more leisurely withdrawal to safety of the distant main body.
>
> Midway to our objective, like the interval at a football match, there was a breathing-space of ten minutes, and according to programme, the halt took place in the middle of a large field. "Jerry," thinking possibly that a weary lot had given up the chase, stood his ground at different points to open fire scarcely two furlongs away. Bullets struck the turf at our feet, or ricochetted off the avenue of small trees which, without affording any cover, marked clearly our resting-line. To make matters worse, shells commenced to crash near by, but fortunately for us, this artillery activity soon ceased. Resuming the offensive under spasmodic bursts of lead from a defiant foe, we arrived outside a farm-house and unceremoniously proceeded to force open the locked door with our rifle butts...since there was no time to lose, we made a hurried departure to follow the onward course over low-lying land. Bursting through a thicket into a garden, our sections came upon the next farm-stead in the line of advance. Breaking into the kitchen after forcibly gaining an entry, Madame, fully alive to the situation, confronted us, and in answer to my sharp inquiry of "Allemande ici?" quickly rushed forward towards me. Gripping my arm, she literally dragged me outside, and pointing across

the yard, said with great excitement: "Allemande parti toute suite!" And as she spoke the back of the last Bosche was to be seen disappearing through the open door-way of the barn. Racing in hot pursuit over the square, then around to the far side of this outhouse, like a game of hide-and-seek, we discovered that the elusive crew of enemy gunners had vanished into the thick undergrowth of a woodland, which extended a considerable distance in the form of a belt. Baulked of our prey once more, it was perhaps a consolation to feel that our exertions were driving them back at top speed.

Skirting the fringe of this spinney, the company advanced in extended order alongside the hedge of a potato field until a fine expanse of countryside came under observation. About six hundred yards ahead where the land assumed a sharp downward trend, a Bosche gun-team appeared in full flight, making for a large farm nestling on the lowland. From a different direction many other enemy stragglers were also to be seen falling back on the same goal... Although our rifles opened out, owing to the previous expenditure of ammunition, the long range and poor visibility, our firing was curtailed. Observing the Germans congregating behind hayricks, we started to career down the slopes towards them. They became alarmed, and carrying their Maxims in a manner to resemble stretchers, started to file across the Kiebeek, a sluggish stream and, incidentally, our objective. At this decided turn in events we were possibly three hundred yards off, and pulling up sharply, brought our Lewis gun into action. After firing a few rounds at the rapidly disappearing figures crossing the plank, owing to hurried manipulation plus some loose soil clogging vital parts, the instrument ceased functioning. The area in front gradually stretched upwards to a high ridge of great strategic importance, and enemy guns on the skyline only waited for the last of their kind to withdraw clear of the stream before springing into activity. Our lively neighbours having disappeared within the folds of the adjoining field, were now preparing for action, and scenting danger, we maintained a quickened pace until with one headlong dive the lot of us vanished from view behind these hayricks. Not a moment too soon, either, for those fiery machines across the narrow strip of water, aroused to anger, rattled forth continuous streams of droning bullets...

By mid-October the manpower situation in the BEF was causing considerable concern. Unlike Ludendorff in the earlier part of the year, Haig and his generals appreciated that the infantry was their most precious resource, and conserved it jealously, minimising casualties through the use of artillery, machine-guns, tanks and aeroplanes. The situation for the Germans was much worse. Many of their divisions were so reduced in number as to be the equivalent of one or two battalions, and they were at times short of both artillery and ammunition for what they had. Counter-attacks became far less frequent, and in any case could be broken up by British artillery. The Official History cites one example, on 17th October, when a group of Germans was seen massing for a counter-attack; after shelling, only one of them reached the British troops. Although machine-gunners continued to be the mainstay of the German army, the defences available to them were feeble compared to those earlier in the war. And if the British were held up at any point by determined resistance, they were now content to stop the attack until the defenders were compelled to withdraw as a result of being outflanked by British advances on either side. There was considerable reluctance now to press attacks home, regardless of casualties. This necessitated a relatively slow advance, and by November, the BEF's problem was to keep contact with an opponent retreating as fast as possible. The Germans could neither afford nor achieve prolonged defence of any point. With disorder at home and in the back areas growing, the German army's position was becoming untenable. While it could have fought on until 1919, gradually withdrawing to Germany, in the end the domestic political situation and the hopeless military prospects led to the request for armistice negotiations, and the end of fighting on 11th November 1918.

Conclusion

The years 1914 to 1918 saw the British army change from a small force of riflemen backed by insubstantial artillery to a large group of five armies, with a force of artillery which could enable it to break through any defensive position it wished. The attack had finally proven stronger than the defence.

This process of change began with the tentative gropings towards a way of breaking the deadlock in 1915, when the BEF was still grossly under-gunned and the infantry almost completely reliant on their rifles. It was not really ready to fight even the small-scale actions of that year, but political pressure which compelled that it be seen actively to be supporting the French, and the generals' desire to press forward meant some attempts at a breakthrough had to be made. Despite the casualties (which were tiny compared to those of succeeding years) valuable lessons were learned, and although gunnery had improved little by the opening of the Battle of the Somme, more firepower was becoming available to the infantry in the shape of Lewis guns, Stokes mortars and grenades. In addition, aerial observation and photography had also begun to have an effect.

The Somme offensive began with the last bombardment in the style of 1915. Given its conspicuous lack of success, it is unsurprising that those parts of the first attack where ground had been gained were studied closely. As a result, the evolution of the creeping barrage was one of the most significant developments of the war, representing as it did the realisation that neutralising and not destructive artillery fire was required. But the technologists had not yet won the day; there was still a tendency to let attacks make do with whatever artillery support was to hand, rather than systematically calculate what was required. And the importance of counter-battery fire was realised only gradually.

The Battle of Arras saw the gunners begin to make the move to a scientific style. Calculations of ammunition requirements were made beforehand, and the barrage and counter-battery work were of greater complexity than anything seen before in the BEF's operations. Had it been intended as a limited affair of one or two days' duration and not an attempt at a breakthrough, it would be considered one of the most successful operations of the war. The infantry too applied new techniques here, not least the passing through of fresh troops once the first wave had gained their objectives. The Battle of Messines saw the process of development continue, and the limited attack in favourable conditions of both weather and terrain was perfected.

Third Ypres saw the BEF attempt to apply the available technology under almost impossible circumstances. Instances, especially towards the end of the battle, of the infantry advancing through thick mud, and the barrage leaving them behind, and at the mercy of German defenders, were depressingly frequent. Given the application of set-piece attacks after the failures in August, and the changes in infantry tactics to counter those of the defenders, far greater results might have been attained, had the offensive been staged elsewhere. But the aim of a breakthrough was nowhere yet realistic. However, the next great technological leap came at Cambrai. The move to predicted fire from well-hidden artillery, and the use of tanks to crush barbed-wire defences in a surprise attack were innovative and successful. Notwithstanding the claims of tank apologists, the former development was of much greater importance than the latter. Given their mechanical shortcomings and vulnerability to artillery fire, it is unlikely that tanks could have been a war-winning weapon in the First World War. Nevertheless, their usefulness in large numbers, and in conjunction with effective small-unit infantry tactics and sophisticated gunnery was considerable.

The inglorious end of the Battle of Cambrai, and the still greater defensive defeats suffered by the BEF in March and April 1918 underlined the problem of an overly hierarchical command structure, and the stifling of initiative it entailed. Interestingly, from the Battle of Amiens onwards, Sir Douglas Haig seemed more inclined than before to listen to his army commanders, and they to note their subordinates' views. While it might be thought that Haig had learned from the disasters earlier in the year, it is far more likely that it was appreciated in the BEF as a whole that specialists had a more and more important role than before, as the emphasis of operations shifted from manpower to firepower, and the BEF's greater stocks of munitions, together with their superior gunnery, gave them an edge over the Germans. Nevertheless, Haig did not force Rawlinson to prolong operations beyond the point where useful results might be obtained at Amiens, as he had done on the Somme in 1916 and at Cambrai and Third Ypres in the following year. In the summer of 1918, he was one of the few people who believed that the war could be won that year, and so he was aware that he needed to husband his resources of manpower. In this his judgement was far better than that of his opposite number, Ludendorff, who wasted manpower in a series of gambles between March and July. The weakened German army was then no match for the complex weapons systems employed by the BEF. Lest it be thought that the part played by the Americans, Belgians and French is played down here, it should be noted that in the final 100 days of the war, the BEF captured 49% of all German troops taken prisoner, and over 40% of the guns. At a terrible price, especially in the preceding years, the British army won its largest land victories ever in 1918.

Glossary and Abbreviations

ADC - Aide de Camp; junior officer acting as the assistant of one more senior.

ANZAC - Australia and New Zealand Army Corps; eventually there were two.

AQMG - Assistant Quartermaster General.

Battery - A group of six guns or howitzers.

BGGS - Brigadier-General, General Staff. The most senior staff officer in a corps; also present in the staffs of higher formations.

BGRA - Brigadier-General, Royal Artillery. The most senior gunner in a corps. See also GOCRA.

Black Maria - see 'Crump.'

Blighty - Slang for Britain. Derived from the Hindi *bilaik*, meaning 'home.'

BM - Brigade Major; the senior staff officer in a brigade.

Boche/Bosche - Slang for the Germans. Derived from the French *alboche*, which seems to be itself derived from a combination of *Allemands* and *tête de boche*, the latter meaning a 'bad lot.'

BQMS - Battery Quartermaster Sergeant; NCO responsible for an artillery battery's logistical affairs.

Buzzer - Device used for sending messages in morse code over the field telegraph.

CCS - Casualty Clearing Station; buildings or tents behind the lines where wounded were operated on and classified according to the severity of their wounds.

CO - Commanding Officer.

Contact Aeroplane - One of the problems commanders in the Great War faced was, in the absence of portable radios, how to find out where their men were during an attack. One solution was to send a contact aeroplane over, to which the infantry would signal, using a variety of means, including Verey lights (q.v.) and large shutters laid on the ground.

CQMS - Company Quartermaster Sergeant. As BQMS, but for an infantry company.

CRA - Commander Royal Artillery; the senior gunner officer attached to a formation. See also GOCRA.

CRE - Commander Royal Engineers; the senior engineer officer attached to a formation.

Crump - A 5.9-inch or heavier German shell (or its explosion). The black smoke produced also led to their being called 'coal-boxes' or 'Jack Johnsons,' after the famous black boxer of the day.

CSM - Company Sergeant Major.

CT - Communication Trench; a trench not facing the enemy lines and used for movement between, for example, the front and support trenches.

DA & QMG - Deputy Adjutant and Quartermaster General; a senior staff post.

Degummed, degumming. The expression used in the Great War to describe being sent home for real or perceived incompetence. Used almost invariably for senior officers, it derives from the French 'degommerer', to unstick. Hence, an alternative form was for a degummed officer to be described as 'degommé'. The Boer War equivalent was to be 'Stellenbosched', since incompetents were sent to the backwater town of Stellenbosch, where they could do no harm. The French Great War version was 'limoger' (adjectival form 'limogé'), since their unstuck officers were consigned to the garrison town of Limoges, far from the front.

Dixie - Large iron pot for boiling and carrying food or tea.

Duckboard - A construction of wood, consisting of two narrow planks about eight feet long with horizontal slats nailed across them. Intended for flooring trenches or making paths across boggy ground, but sometimes used for firewood or roofing dugouts (q.v.).

Dugout/Dug-out - Term for various types of shelter, ranging from a hole scraped in the side of a trench ('cubby-hole') to a deep dugout, ten or more feet underground and possibly walled with wood and provided with sleeping accommodation and electric light. Captured German dugouts, if not badly damaged, were viewed as most luxurious. Also used to refer to officers who had left the army before the war, and rejoined owing to the shortage of trained officers in 1914-15.

Enfilade - To fire down a trench or at a row of men lengthways, rather than crosswise. A particularly lethal way of firing, since it is much less likely that bullets or shells will fall short or over their target. In addition, the target itself is denser - a row of 50 men, one deep, is equivalent to a column of 50 when enfiladed.

Firestep - The trenches, in order to provide protection, were usually deeper than a man's height. In order for sentries or troops at 'stand to' (q.v.) to be able to fire upon an enemy, the front wall of the trench had a raised portion for them to stand on. This was the firestep.

Flying Pig - A type of trench mortar bomb.

FOO - Forward Observation Officer for artillery batteries.

GHQ - General Headquarters; the headquarters of the Commander in Chief.

GOC - General Officer Commanding.

GOCRA - General Officer Commanding Royal Artillery. It was realised in 1915 that the artillery adviser to a corps commander needed more executive power, in order to co-ordinate its growing quantity of artillery more effectively (and especially heavy artillery, which largely operated at corps level). Therefore the post of GOCRA was created; the title was changed to BGRA in May 1916, but restored to GOCRA in December of that year.

GS Wagon - General Service Wagon; standard horse- or mule-drawn cart used for transporting supplies etc.

GSO1 - General Staff Officer, grade one.

Gun - High velocity artillery piece with a flat trajectory; rarely fired at an angle greater than 20°.

HAC - The Honourable Artillery Company, the oldest Territorial unit in the army. It was composed of both infantry and gunners in the Great War.

Howitzer - Artillery piece firing a heavier projectile at a lower velocity than a gun of similar calibre, and at a higher angle. Could be fired with a variable charge.

HQ - Headquarters.

Jam Tin Bomb - Improvised grenade (bomb, in Great War parlance); dangerous to both friend and foe.

Knife Rest - Horizontal bar, 25-30 feet long, with cross-pieces about three feet long at each end, and barbed wire strung between them.

Landwehr - German reservist troops.

Lewis gun - The standard light machine-gun of the British army; although it weighed 26lb (unloaded), it could be fired by one man, but several more were required to carry drums of ammunition. It had an unfortunate tendency to jam in dirty conditions, of which there were no shortage on the Western Front.

Maxim - A type of heavy machine gun favoured by the German army, although the Vickers gun was sometimes referred to as the 'Vickers Maxim.'

Minenwerfer/Minnie - German trench mortar.

MO - Medical Officer.

MGRA - Major-General, Royal Artillery; the senior gunner in an Army.

MTOC - Motor Transport Officer Commanding; officer in charge of a lorry park or the like.

NCO - Non-commissioned Officer, such as a corporal or sergeant.

OC - Officer Commanding.

OP - Observation Post.

ORs - Other ranks; soldiers who are not officers, including NCOs but not warrant officers.

Picquet, piquet - Soldier on outpost sentry duty; or stake or similar contrivance to support barbed wire.

RA - Royal Artillery.

RAMC - Royal Army Medical Corps; also known as 'Rob All My Comrades' owing to the tendency of orderlies to steal from sleeping or unconscious patients.

RE - Royal Engineers.

Register - Technical term used by gunners, meaning to locate a target by means of each gun in a battery firing ranging rounds. A FOO (q.v.) would inform the battery of what adjustments to their range etc. were required in order to hit the target.

RFC - Royal Flying Corps; became the RAF on 1st April 1918.

Rfmn. - Abbreviation for Rifleman, the name for a private soldier in 'Rifle' regiments.

RSM - Regimental Sergeant-Major.

SAA - Small Arms Ammunition, i.e. for rifles, pistols and machine-guns.

Shrapnel - Type of artillery shell filled with small lead balls, which would spray forwards and downwards with lethal effect, upon the shell bursting.

Stand To - Period when troops in the front line were required to man the firestep (q.v.) of their trench, fully armed, in case of enemy attack. Routinely done at dawn and nightfall every day.

Stick Bomb - Type of German hand grenade with a wooden handle attached, so that it could be thrown further.

Stokes mortar - Light mortar, consisting of a smooth-bore tube, resting on a baseplate, and supported by a bipod.

Traverse - The trenches were not straight ditches, since this would have made them far too vulnerable to enfilade fire (q.v.). Instead, they periodically had traverses built in. These were protrusions of earth or sandbags into the trench, giving trench lines a crenellated appearance when viewed from the air. They also had the function of limiting the effects of shells, mortar bombs, etc. when they landed in the trench.

Uhlan - German lancer, though the term was often applied to any German cavalry.

Verey Light - A type of flare, fired from a brass pistol and used to illuminate No-Man's-Land at night, or for signalling purposes.

Vickers gun - The standard heavy machine-gun of the British army. Unlike the Lewis, the Vickers was water cooled, and given that it also weighed over 88lb, it was far less mobile. Its use of ammunition in belts meant that it could be fired for far longer than the Lewis, and it had a greater range. However, it required a team (in theory) of ten men to carry the gun, its mounting, water and ammunition.

WO - Warrant Officer; senior level of NCO, such as RSM or Battn QMS.

Bibliography

The author and publishers gratefully acknowledge the following source works:

Primary sources

[Bidder (Major H.F.)] 'Orex' *Three Chevrons*. Bodley Head. 1919.

Buckley (Francis) *Q.6.A. and other places: Recollections of 1916, 1917, 1918*. Spottiswoode. 1920.

Clapham (H.S.) *Mud and Khaki: The Memories of an Incomplete Soldier*. Hutchinson. 1930.

Coleman (Frederick) *From Mons to Ypres with French: A Personal Narrative*. Sampson Low. 1916.

Dolbey (R.V.) *A Regimental Surgeon in War and Prison*. Murray. 1917.

Dolden (A.Stuart) *Cannon Fodder: An Infantryman's Life on the Western Front 1914-1918*. Blandford Press. 1980. Copyright by Blandford Press, 1980. Extracts reproduced by kind permission of Cassell Plc.

Dugdale (Captain Geoffrey) *"Langemarck" and "Cambrai": A War Narrative 1914-18*. Shrewsbury. 1932.

['E.A.F.'] *Vermelles: Notes on the Western Front by a Chaplain*. Scottish Chronicle. 1918.

Eden (Sir Anthony) *Another World 1897-1917*. Allen Lane. 1976.

Fraser-Tytler (Lt.Col. N.) *Field Guns in France*. Hutchinson. 1922.

Gibbs (Sir Philip) *Realities of War*. Heinemann. 1920.

Graham (Major Francis) *Letters from the Front August 1914-March 1918*. The Harrow School Bookshop. nd.

Gregory (Henry) *Never Again: A Diary of the Great War*. Arthur Stockwell. 1934.

[Hay (Captain M.V.)] 'An Exchanged Officer' *Wounded and a Prisoner of War*. Blackwoods. 1916.

Housman (L.) Ed: *War Letters of Fallen Englishmen*. Gollancz. 1930.

Jeffrey (Jeffrey E.) *Servants of the Guns*. Smith, Elder. 1917.

Lloyd (T.) *The Blazing Trail of Flanders*. Heath Cranton. 1933.

[Smith (Aubrey)] 'A Rifleman' *Four Years on the Western Front*. Odham's. 1922.

Smith (Captain H.Raymond) *A Soldier's Diary: Sidelights on the Great War 1914-1918*. Evesham: The "Journal" Press. 1940.

[Symons (Lt.Col. F.A.)] 'Royal Field Leech' *The Tale of a Casualty Clearing Station*. Blackwood. 1917.

Tennyson (Lionel Lord) *From Verse to Worse*. Cassell. 1933.

Watson (Major W.H.L.) *A Company of Tanks*. Blackwood. 1920.

Secondary sources and suggestions for further reading

Aston (John) and Duggan (L.M.) *The History of the 12th (Bermondsey) Battalion, East Surrey Regiment*. Union Press. 1936.

Barnett (Correlli) *The Swordbearers: Studies in Supreme Command in the First World War*. Eyre and Spottiswoode. 1963.

Barrie (Alexander) *War Underground. The Tunnellers of the Great War*. Tom Donovan. 1988.

Baynes (John) *Morale: A Study of Men and Courage: The Second Scottish Rifles at the Battle of Neuve Chapelle 1915*. Cassell. 1967.

Beckett (Ian F.W.) and Simpson (Keith) eds. *A Nation in Arms*. Tom Donovan. 1990.

Bidwell (Shelford) *Gunners at War*. Arms and Armour Press. 1970.

Bidwell (Shelford) and Graham (Dominick) *Fire-Power: British Army Weapons and Theories of War, 1904-45*. Allen and Unwin. 1982.

Cooper (Bryan) *The Ironclads of Cambrai*. Pan Books. 1970.

Edmonds (Br.-Gen. Sir J.E.) et al. *History of the Great War: Military Operations France and Belgium*. 14 Vols, HMSO. 1922-48.

Essame (H.) *The Battle for Europe 1918*. Batsford. 1972.

Farrar-Hockley (A.H.) *Death of an Army*. Arthur Barker. 1967.

Farrar-Hockley (A.H.) *Goughie*. Hart-Davis, MacGibbon. 1975.

Graham (Dominick) and Bidwell (Shelford) *Coalitions, Politicians and Generals*. Brassey's. 1993.

Griffith (Paddy) *Battle Tactics of the Western Front*. Yale University Press. 1994.

Liddell Hart (B.H.) *The Real War 1914-1918*. Faber and Faber. 1930.

McCarthy (Chris) *The Somme: The Day-by-Day Account*. Arms and Armour Press. 1993.

Middlebrook (Martin) *The First Day on the Somme*. Allen Lane. 1971.

Powell (Geoffrey) *Plumer - The Soldiers' General*. Leo Cooper. 1990.

Prior (Robin) and Wilson (Trevor) *Command on the Western Front*. Blackwell. 1992.

Seymour (Br.-Gen. Wm.W.) *The History of the Rifle Brigade in the War of 1914 to 1919. Volume 2*. Rifle Brigade Club Ltd. 1936.

Simpson (Andy) *Hot Blood and Cold Steel: Life and Death in the Trenches of the First World War*. Tom Donovan. 1993.

Sixsmith (Maj.-Gen. E.K.G.) *British Generalship in the Twentieth Century*. Arms and Armour Press. 1970.

Terraine (John) *Douglas Haig: The Educated Soldier*. Hutchinson. 1963.

Terraine (John) *To Win a War: 1918, the year of victory*. Sidgwick and

Jackson. 1978.

Thornton (Lt.-Col. L.H.) and Fraser (Pamela) *The Congreves Father and Son*. John Murray. 1930.

Travers (Tim) *How the War was Won. Command and Technology in the British Army on the Western Front 1917-1918*. Routledge. 1992.

Travers (Tim) *The Killing Ground: The British Army, the Western Front and the Emergence of Modern Warfare 1900-1918*. Allen and Unwin. 1987.

Tuchman (Barbara) *The Guns of August*. Macmillan. 1962.

Williams (Jeffrey) *Byng of Vimy: General and Governor General*. Leo Cooper/Secker and Warburg. 1983.

Woolf (Leon) *In Flanders Fields: The 1917 Campaign*. Longmans, Green. 1960.

Index

UNIVERSITY
OF
GLASGOW
LIBRARY